The Blood of the Everlasting Covenant

By Larry Chkoreff
Original 2006
Version 5.7 2017
ISBN 978-0-9676731-8-9

Published by International School of the Bible (ISOB), Marietta, Georgia, U.S.A.

Cover art by Tracey Diaz.

Forward

God's original blood relationship still creates a craving, a longing inside of us for the blood covenant with God.

In spite of the fact that Adam became disconnected with God, he and his descendants maintained a deep craving for that original connection. I believe that craving has been passed down through the generations in much the same way that Adam's sin has been passed down.

I believe that in each of us exists a craving for that blood connection that Adam once had. I believe that the more primitive and even Eastern cultures, which rely more upon their intuition than their intellect, sense that craving for the blood covenant in a greater way. God's purpose is to continually change us into "children," so that we may sense that craving.

In 1 Corinthians 1:18-2:5 the Apostle Paul said that he would preach only the Cross and that he would not use eloquent words of worldly wisdom. He indicated that the power was in the Cross, or in the blood of Jesus. His experience in Athens (Acts 17) showed that he was somewhat frustrated with arguing with the intellectuals.

My personal experience, and the experience of some people that I know, has been that as we read about the blood covenant, the knowledge bypasses our intellect and goes directly into our hearts. Another way to put it is that the blood covenant revelation is for the right side of our brain and not so much for the left side. The left side of the brain deals more with logic and intellect. The right side of the brain is more about the "heart language, or the creative side."

Adam and Eve chose to eat from the Tree of Knowledge of Good and Evil, which I submit was their intellect. The Tree of Life is the Word of God.

I know so many Christians who "know" so much in their heads, but their hearts are lacking the authentic and true relationship with Jesus.

As you read these chapters about The Blood of The Everlasting Covenant, simply allow the stories to soak into your soul. I submit that you will soon obtain a more accurate self-identity in Jesus. You will see yourself as God sees you, a new creation in Him, totally recreated and reborn to a new race, which has dominion over your spiritual enemies. You will see bondages, habits, addictions, depression, oppression, hopelessness and fear, all be displaced by the love of God.

Acknowledgements

I want to thank my precious wife Carol for her help and encouragement in doing this book.

Carol encouraged me to actually create this book. Originally, these chapters were lessons that we taught in our Bible class at Mount Paran North Church of God. Carol continued to influence me to assemble them into a book.

Thanks to our friends who performed some very detailed proof reading.

Thanks to Mount Paran North Church of God who made it possible for us to bring these lessons to the wonderful group of people in our class.

Thanks to all the people in our Overcomers Bible Class who continually encouraged us to bring these lessons to print, and who are demonstrating in their lives the fruit from studying them.

2006

Table of Contents

Introduction

Do you find yourself in the "fires of life?" Is life overwhelming for you? The God who created the entire universe is offering to exchange places with you through a blood covenant.

Daniel chapter 3 contains a story about King Nebuchadnezzar. The King made an image of himself and ordered that all people should worship him through the image. The decree went out that whoever would not worship this statue would be cast into a fiery furnace. The three Hebrews – Shadrach, Meshach, and Abed-Nego – refused to worship the king through his image-statue.

Daniel 3:16-18 says,

> *16 "Shadrach, Meshach, and Abed-Nego answered and said to the king, 'O Nebuchadnezzar, we have no need to answer you in this matter.*
>
> *17 If that* is the case, *our God whom we serve is able to deliver us from the burning fiery furnace, and He will deliver us from your hand, O king.*
>
> *18 But if not, let it be known to you, O king, that we do not serve your gods, nor will we worship the gold image which you have set up.'"*

The Hebrews used fire for their worship. However, their fire memorialized the blood covenant sacrifice. Their fire killed the innocent lamb thus saving their own lives.

What happened was no less than a miracle.

Daniel 3:19-25 says,

> *19 "Then Nebuchadnezzar was full of fury, and the expression on his face changed toward Shadrach, Meshach, and Abed-Nego. He spoke and commanded that they heat the furnace seven times more than it was usually heated.*
>
> *20 And he commanded certain mighty men of valor who were in his army to bind Shadrach, Meshach, and Abed-Nego, and cast them into the burning fiery furnace.*

21 Then these men were bound in their coats, their trousers, their turbans, and their other garments, and were cast into the midst of the burning fiery furnace.

22 Therefore, because the king's command was urgent, and the furnace exceedingly hot, the flame of the fire killed those men who took up Shadrach, Meshach, and Abed-Nego.

23 And these three men, Shadrach, Meshach, and Abed-Nego, fell down bound into the midst of the burning fiery furnace.

24 Then King Nebuchadnezzar was astonished; and he rose in haste and spoke, saying to his counselors, 'Did we not cast three men bound into the midst of the fire?' They answered and said to the king, 'True, O king.'

25 'Look!' he answered, 'I see four men loose, walking in the midst of the fire; and they are not hurt, and the form of the fourth is like the Son of God.'"

The furnace contained four men, but only three came out. Daniel 3:26-27 says,

26 "Then Nebuchadnezzar went near the mouth of the burning fiery furnace and spoke, saying, 'Shadrach, Meshach, and Abed-Nego, servants of the Most High God, come out, and come here.' Then Shadrach, Meshach, and Abed-Nego came from the midst of the fire.

27 And the satraps, administrators, governors, and the king's counselors gathered together, and they saw these men on whose bodies the fire had no power; the hair of their head was not singed nor were their garments affected, and the smell of fire was not on them."

The fourth Man in the fire was God Himself, the Son of God, and He stayed in the furnace and took the death penalty for the other three. But as we know, He was resurrected after three days!

He will do the same for you! Whatever it is that has put your life into bondage, into a prison, or in torment or hopelessness, God will allow that to come upon Himself on your behalf so that you can be free. He will give you His resurrected life!

These three Hebrews were made righteous by faith.
It says in Romans 3:23 that all have sinned, including these three Hebrew boys.

Romans 6:22-23 says,

> *22 "But now having been set free from sin, and having become slaves of God, you have your fruit to holiness, and the end, everlasting life.*
> *23 For the wages of sin* is *death, but the gift of God* is *eternal life in Christ Jesus our Lord."*

These boys were, as Daniel chapter 3 says, "clothed in other garments."

Isaiah 61:10 says,

> *10 "I will greatly rejoice in the LORD, My soul shall be joyful in my God; For He has clothed me with the garments of salvation, He has covered me with the robe of righteousness, as a bridegroom decks himself with ornaments, and as a bride adorns herself with her jewels."*

The reason they did not burn was that Jesus took on their sinful nature and burned in their stead. They took on Jesus' righteousness and as a result, could not be injured.

The result had eternal value, much more than just the deliverance of these three men. King Nebuchadnezzar sent out decrees worldwide that the Hebrew God should be worshipped. God's fame was made known by this king throughout all of the inhabited earth, at least as far as his kingdom reached.

Daniel 3: 28-30 says,

> *28 "Nebuchadnezzar spoke, saying, 'Blessed be the God of Shadrach, Meshach, and Abed-Nego, who sent His Angel and delivered His servants who trusted in*

Him, and they have frustrated the king's word, and yielded their bodies, that they should not serve nor worship any god except their own God!

29 Therefore I make a decree that any people, nation, or language which speaks anything amiss against the God of Shadrach, Meshach, and Abed-Nego shall be cut in pieces, and their houses shall be made an ash heap; because there is no other God who can deliver like this.'

30 Then the king promoted Shadrach, Meshach, and Abed-Nego in the province of Babylon."

That is the concept of a blood covenant.

Two parties exchange places. If you need to exchange places with someone, if you need a new start in life, a new birth as it may be, read on.

As you discover the love of God in the Blood of the Everlasting Covenant, you may be brought to a place where you begin to worship Him as these Hebrews did. You will discover then, as Jerry Seville once said, "If you don't bow, you won't burn." Your life will not even "smell like smoke," and your influence will make God known to others.

You will also, progressively, begin to understand better who you really are in Christ. The blood covenant image will bypass your mind and go directly into your heart. This will give you an accurate image of who you really are. It will dispel the lie that attaches itself to you, telling you that you are unworthy. As you see your new self-image, you will simply find yourself living a different life, no longer desiring to do those things that are unpleasing to God. The next result will be that the power of God in you will do warfare against the satanic powers in your realm of influence. Not only will you be delivered, but more importantly, God's plan to reach others will be manifested through your life.

Chapter 1
Religion or Blood?

"Then Jesus said to them, 'Most assuredly, I say to you, unless you eat the flesh of the Son of Man and drink His blood, you have no life in you. Whoever eats My flesh and drinks My blood has eternal life, and I will raise him up at the last day. For My flesh is food indeed, and My blood is drink indeed. He who eats My flesh and drinks My blood abides in Me, and I in him'" (John 6:53-56).

Have you ever been denied a miracle?

As a believer perhaps there have been desperate times in your life when you felt it would be appropriate for God to give you a miracle. You read about His miracle working power in the Bible, you read that He loves you, now you want to see it in your circumstances. Putting these two assumptions together, you ask God for a miracle, and you expect Him to give it to you. Sometimes He does, but sometimes, perhaps even more often, He does not.

What are you to believe? Where is God in your affliction?

Perhaps we can learn from the events recorded in John chapter 6. Jesus had just supernaturally fed more than 5,000 poor and needy people in the setting of a third world country. He took five loaves of bread and two fish and did a miracle of increase that would astonish anybody. They thought for sure that this was the prophet that Moses had spoken of, the one who would again provide manna from Heaven.

John 6:15 says,

15 "Therefore when Jesus perceived that they were about to come and take Him by force to make Him king, He departed again to the mountain by Himself alone."

The disciples entered their boat and crossed the sea. Jesus walked on the water, and they arrived to the other side together. But the crowd who had been fed looked for Jesus the next morning hoping for another miracle. They finally found Him.

Jesus refused their request.

John 6:26-27 says,

26 "Jesus answered them and said, 'Most assuredly, I say to you, you seek Me, not because you saw the signs, but because you ate of the loaves and were filled.

27 Do not labor for the food which perishes, but for the food which endures to everlasting life, which the Son of Man will give you, because God the Father has set His seal on Him.'"

Jesus admonished them to turn their efforts to what God requires. He knew that feeding them again would simply be another short-term fix, but it would not solve their true problem, which resided in their hearts and souls. Jesus wants us to prosper. Jesus wants to meet our needs, but from the inside out, not from the outside in!

John 6:29 says,

29 "Jesus answered and said to them, 'This is the work of God, that you believe in Him whom He sent.'"

Then Jesus started a conversation that really caught them off guard. He has a way of doing that. We may be thinking about a material or earthly need, and He turns our attention to the real issue.

John 6:31-35 says,

31 "Our fathers ate the manna in the desert; as it is written, 'He gave them bread from heaven to eat.'

32 Then Jesus said to them, 'Most assuredly, I say to you, Moses did not give you the bread from heaven, but My Father gives you the true bread from heaven.

33 For the bread of God is He who comes down from heaven and gives life to the world.'

34 Then they said to Him, 'Lord, give us this bread always.'

35 And Jesus said to them, 'I am the bread of life. He who comes to Me shall never hunger, and he who believes in Me shall never thirst.'"

Their response was interesting.

John 6:41 says,

41 "The Jews then complained about Him, because He said, 'I am the bread which came down from heaven.'"

Then He took them even deeper down His road of surprises when He said, "I am the living bread which came down from heaven. If anyone eats of this bread, he will live forever; and the bread that I shall give is My flesh, which I shall give for the life of the world" (John 6:51), and "He who eats My flesh and drinks My blood abides in Me, and I in him" (John 6:56).

Jesus was offering them a blood covenant with the Maker of the Universe. Jesus was using mystical blood covenant language in this conversation.

This is what He offers you and me. Can you just imagine? The infinite Almighty God, sinless and holy offers to exchange places with you and me, mere created and sinful people! He knew that having a blood covenant would make these people one with Him. They would abide in Him and He would abide in them. He knew that if they accepted the covenant that all their needs would be cared for. Which would you rather have, a miracle to take care of today's problem, or a covenant of blood with Deity?

John 6:60 says,

60 "Therefore many of His disciples, when they heard this, *said, 'This is a hard saying; who can understand it?'"*

Jesus persisted and even made things sound more difficult. He asked them how much more they would be offended if He left and they could not even catch Him to eat His flesh and drink His blood. He was speaking of His crucifixion and resurrection (John

6:61-62). It is human nature to desire a god or an idol that the natural eye can see.

Here is the major point.

John 6:63 says,

63 "It is the Spirit who gives life; the flesh profits nothing. The words that I speak to you are spirit, and they *are life."*

In other words He was saying, "You don't have to actually become a cannibal and drink My blood, but if you want a blood covenant with Me you will eat My Word, because My Word and I are one. My Words are supernatural. The more of the Word you obtain, the more of My blood you receive!" Covenants are made with words. In this case the Word replaces blood. Yes, Jesus shed His blood, and that blood is transferred to you through His Word. You have an invitation to enter into the blood covenant with the Maker, God Himself. All He has is yours, provided, of course, that all you have is His!

"Sorry, Jesus, without a miracle I am out of here!"

John 6:66 says,

66 "From that time *many of His disciples went back and walked with Him no more."*

Some disciples stayed.

John 6:67-69 says,

67 "Then Jesus said to the twelve, 'Do you also want to go away?'

68 But Simon Peter answered Him, 'Lord, to whom shall we go? You have the words of eternal life.

69 Also we have come to believe and know that You are the Christ, the Son of the living God.'"

Jesus, through the blood covenant and exchange that took place, gave us His resurrection power so that we could apply it here on earth on His behalf, in His name!

Quick fixes and miracles will not build your character; they will make you dependent slaves.

Psalm 119:67 says,

67 "Before I was afflicted I went astray, but now I keep Your word."

God created us to be fed from the inside, not from the outside. Remember He said in Matthew 6:28 that lilies are clothed better than Solomon because they have life inside of them. Our provisions and all of our needs, emotional, spiritual and physical are to come from the life of God on the inside of us.

Blood covenants are embedded in the nature of mankind. Historically almost every culture in the world has recognized the ritual of the blood covenant. It is only in recent civilized history that mankind has become so "educated" that they have reasoned their way out of the significance of the blood covenant.

Contracts have replaced covenants in much of today's civilized world. A contract is a document that states an agreement between the parties and then lays out what happens when the contract is broken. It is altogether "selfish." It assumes that the parties will break the agreement.

A covenant is the basis of relationship, an expression of love between the parties. It carries the spirit of generosity, sacrifice, and death to a self-centered life. It carries the spirit of resurrection to an abundant life, love and intimacy. It is a lifelong commitment to each party wherein each party gives up its right to its own possessions, strengths and resources. *In a covenant relationship, each party dies to his/her own personal interests, and puts the interest of the other party in first place!*

Covenants are usually made between unequal parties. In a primitive culture one party may have great expertise in agriculture and sees itself as totally defenseless militarily. The other party may have great military strength, but is having a difficult time feeding its people. The covenant they make in blood contains those mutual promises to care for the other's weakness. The penalty for failing to do so is death!

The American Indian attacked the white man even when the Indians knew it would be to their death. Why? Because the white man made covenant with them and broke it. The Indian had a spiritual obligation to seek death. That meant more to them than their own destruction.

We must allow God to renew our minds to covenant thinking in order to really understand and appreciate Him the most. If we do not understand covenant thinking we will not appreciate the Bible, its power, its authority and God's love. We will not understand the depth of God's love because we will continually judge His love from our own perspective.

Covenant love is like none other.

In Hebrew language it is expressed as *checed*, which is commonly translated as mercy or *lovingkindness* as in Psalm 23.

Psalm 23:6 (KJV) says,

> *6 "Surely goodness and mercy (checed) shall follow me all the days of my life: and I will dwell in the house of the LORD for ever."*

In the New Testament Greek the word is *agape*. It indicates an aching love just looking for someone to pour on.

It is expressed in the following Scripture.

Ephesians 2:4-7 (Amplified Bible) says,

> *4 "But God – so rich is He in His mercy! Because of and in order to satisfy the great and wonderful and intense love with which He loved us,*
>
> *5 Even when we were dead (slain) by [our own] shortcomings and trespasses, He made us alive together in fellowship and in union with Christ; [He gave us the very life of Christ Himself, the same new life with which He quickened Him, for] it is by grace (His favor and mercy which you did not deserve) that you are saved (delivered from judgment and made partakers of Christ's salvation)].*
>
> *6 And He raised us up together with Him and made us sit down together [giving us joint seating with Him]*

in the heavenly sphere [by virtue of our being] in Christ Jesus (the Messiah, the Anointed One).

7 He did this that He might clearly demonstrate through the ages to come the immeasurable (limitless, surpassing) riches of His free grace (His unmerited favor) in [His] kindness and goodness of heart toward us in Christ Jesus."

A blood covenant defined.

[1] *"A rite by which two persons absorb each the other's blood, either by drinking or by transfusion to the veins, whereby they become bound to each other in even a closer connection than that of brotherhood. It prevails in many countries, civilized and uncivilized, and may be traced back to extreme antiquity. It existed in the rites and literature of the ancient Egyptians, and is frequently alluded to in the Bible. Dr. H. Clay Trumbull, who has made a scientific examination of the subject, holds that its origin is in the universally dominative primitive convictions that the blood is the life; that the heart, as the blood-fountain, is the very soul of every personality; that blood-transfer is soul-transfer; that blood-sharing, human or divine-human, secures an interunion of natures; and that a union of the human nature with the divine is the highest ultimate attainment reached out after by the most primitive as well as by the most enlightened mind of humanity. With savage and barbarous peoples the rite lies at the foundations of cannibalism; it is the motive of sacrifices, in which the animal is offered to the god as a substitute for the human blood.*

What would you choose?

---

[1] Walsh, William S. *Curiosities of Popular Customs* - Copyright 1897 by J.B. Lippincott Company Copyright 1925 by Katharine Walsh - Main >> Cultures & Beliefs >> Christianity http://hometown.aol.com/

Which would you rather experience, a miracle that will fix your problems, or the miracle of a blood covenant with the Creator of the universe? Don't be like those disciples who walked away from Jesus as recorded in John chapter 6. Many Christians do so. They don't really walk away in their minds, but they do not cherish the Word of God as the essence of the relationship.

Isaiah 53:3 says,

> *3 "He is despised and rejected by men, A Man of sorrows and acquainted with grief. And we hid, as it were,* our *faces from Him; He was despised, and we did not esteem Him."*

Who is the *Him* in this Scripture? Jesus. Who is Jesus? The Word of God! *Despise* means to consider worthless. Why do so many Christians despise the Word of God and consider it of little value?

We avoid the curses in our lives and invoke the blessings when we hear and obey the Word.

Deuteronomy 28:2 (KJV) says,

> *2 "And all these blessings shall come on thee, and overtake thee, if thou shalt hearken unto the voice of the LORD thy God."*

Hearken means to listen to, to understand, to yield to and obey.

Deuteronomy 28:15 (KJV) says,

> *15 "But it shall come to pass, if thou wilt not hearken unto the voice of the LORD thy God, to observe to do all his commandments and his statutes which I command thee this day; that all these curses shall come upon thee, and overtake thee."*

When you need a miracle and you don't see one manifesting, pursue the blood covenant by being diligent to hear the Word of God. Do whatever it takes to stay in the Word until that logos, the general Word of God, becomes rhema, the personal Word of God coming directly from the lips of Jesus to your heart. You will become addicted to that relationship.

I pray that you will be impacted in a way even deeper than having your needs met. I pray that when you realize that you indeed have a blood covenant with the Creator, the One who has existed forever, that you would experience a sense of awe and reverence of what you now contain. You have become the container of Deity. This should be enough to make anybody get their minds off of themselves and their temporal needs, and onto Jesus, God Almighty!

It is not just about you!

I heard a story about a psychiatrist who was counseling with a lady. She was in her fifth session. The psychiatrist said, "I am going to write you a prescription that will totally heal your problem." She said, "Okay, fantastic. Let me see it." The doctor handed the lady what he had written. She said, "This is absurd. This is shameful. What do you mean taking my hard earned money and giving me something like this? This says to check into a nice hotel at Niagara Falls. Then I should go stand at the base of the Falls for four days and just watch it. How will this help me?" The doctor said, "For five weeks you have told me about yourself, your dreams, your problems, how others have made you feel, how others have hurt you, and so on. You just need to see that there is something bigger than you and get your mind off of yourself."

Now go ahead and give Jesus your words, and absorb His blood covenant Word. Stand in awe of what you receive, and you will never be the same!

Chapter 2
Adam's Words of Death

Learn from Adam's story.
Adam had the blood connection with God but he lost it. His words became perverted. Now God has a plan of restoration that is based upon God breathed words spoken by Him to man and by man to this world for restoration. When I use the name *Adam*, I am not limiting that to the original man Adam, but to Adam, the Adamic race including you and me before God gave us the new birth.

Genesis 2:7 (KJV) says,

7 "And the LORD God formed man of the dust of the ground, and breathed into his nostrils the breath of life; and man became a living soul."

The Lord worked like a potter, a very intelligent and scientific one, to form Adam from the earth's substance. Then somehow the Lord breathed His very own life into Adam. The result was that Adam received God's spirit and the by-product was Adam's soul. Adam must have had God's perfect blood in him, although Adam was not deity as Jesus was when He became flesh.

Adam was originally given dominion to rule the earth by his words.

Genesis 1:26-28 says,

26 "Then God said, 'Let Us make man in Our image, according to Our likeness; let them have dominion over the fish of the sea, over the birds of the air, and over the cattle, over all the earth and over every creeping thing that creeps on the earth.'

27 So God created man in His own image; in the image of God He created him; male and female He created them.

28 Then God blessed them, and God said to them, 'Be fruitful and multiply; fill the earth and subdue it; have dominion over the fish of the sea, over the birds of the air, and over every living thing that moves on the earth.'"

Adam, however, was instructed to not work by himself, but to be co-laborers with God. God instructed Adam to live by the Word of God, the Tree of Life. He warned Adam to not depend upon his own intellect, his own will and emotions, but to only rely on what He, God, said.

God's plan was to fellowship with Adam, speak His Words to him, and have Adam carry out the plans and ideas. Adam was to respond by working and obeying the Word, but also by speaking it as well. Adam and Eve were designed to have a very close intimate friendship with God Himself. For some time they did. Most religious people cannot imagine this. The fruit of this continual intimacy was to be Adam speaking God's Words over the earth. Earth was designed to be ruled by the words of man. Everything in and on the earth responds to man's words.

God warned Adam that he would die if he disobeyed. He did disobey and died spiritually immediately, and over 900 years later he died physically. It took his body that long to "learn how to die." It was God's grace that Adam did not live forever in his fallen condition. The earth began to respond as well; the natural order of things began to corrupt. Storms began to wreck havoc on nature, animals which were previously friendly, became evil and dangerous.

The earth is ruled by words spoken by a human being.

Psalm 8:2-6 says,

"2 Out of the mouth of babes and nursing infants You have ordained strength, Because of Your enemies, That You may silence the enemy and the avenger.

3 When I consider Your heavens, the work of Your fingers, The moon and the stars, which You have ordained,

4 What is man that You are mindful of him, And the son of man that You visit him?

5 For You have made him a little lower than the angels [elohiym - God], And You have crowned him with glory and honor.

6 You have made him to have dominion over the works of Your hands; You have put all things under his feet,"

The two "trees" that represented Adam's instructions were the Tree of Life, which is the Word of God, and the Tree of Knowledge of Good and Evil, which is human reasoning without God being involved. As long as Adam stayed in fellowship with the Lord God, heard His Words, obeyed them and spoke them as words of dominion over the earth and every creeping thing, then all would be well. The life connection between God and Adam would have been maintained. However, Adam began to speak his own words that were formed while out of fellowship with God, and then his descendants began to speak Satan's words. Since then, the world has been under the power of the prince of darkness.

Eve's words were wrong.

Eve said that God said, "but of the fruit of the tree which is in the midst of the garden, God has said, 'You shall not eat it, nor shall you touch it, lest you die'" (Genesis 3:3). God never said not to touch it, instead He said, "but of the tree of the knowledge of good and evil you shall not *eat*, for in the day that you *eat* of it you shall surely die" (Genesis 2:17). Was Satan really to blame?

Adam began to speak words of his own and of Satan's origin and the earth responded.

In the previous chapter we saw how Jesus gave us the key to re-establishing the blood covenant with God through His Word. This is what Adam lost, and that was through the fruit of Adam's words coming through the abundance of his heart.

Adam and Eve immediately became "religious" when they knew that they were out of fellowship with God. What do I mean by religious? First, they began to blame others, and failed to take responsibility. They began to speak the words that originated from their own minds, rather than the Word of God. Then they tried to make amends by using fig leaves.

Genesis 3:7 says,

> *7 "Then the eyes of both of them were opened, and they knew that they were naked; and they sewed fig leaves together and made themselves coverings."*

All of Scripture, especially the words of Jesus, warns us, that our negative words are powerful for evil. Not only do they create evil in our own lives, but also in the lives of those around us. We will be accountable for our words at the judgment. Why? Because our words can create and also they can destroy!

Careless with words!

Being careless with our words will even keep God's presence from being real in our lives. Psalm 15:1 asks the questions, "Who will abide in Your tabernacle? Who may dwell in Your holy hill?" Then the next few verses lay out the requirements. They include walking uprightly, working righteousness, speaking the truth in one's heart, not backbiting with the tongue, not doing evil to one's neighbor, and not taking up a reproach against his friend. Backbiting can be likened to gossip and taking up a reproach can be likened to listening to and receiving gossip.

Colossians 4:6 says,

> *6* "Let *your speech always* be *with grace, seasoned with salt, that you may know how you ought to answer each one."*

Death and life.

Satan's name in the New Testament actually means *slanderer*. James says in chapter 3 of his epistle, that the tongue sets the whole course of nature on fire, like the fire of hell. He says that, in effect, the tongue rules the entire brain center, and therefore the entire person. Science has discovered that indeed the speech center has dominion over the entire brain.

Proverbs 18:21 says,

21 "Death and life are *in the power of the tongue, and those that love it will eat its fruit."*

Romans 4:17 says,

"17 (as it is written, "I have made you [Abraham] a father of many nations") in the presence of Him whom he believed--God, who gives life to the dead and calls those things which do not exist as though they did;"

Mark 11:22-24 says,

22 "So Jesus answered and said to them, 'Have faith in God [literally means, "have the faith of God"].

23 For assuredly, I say to you, whoever says to this mountain, 'Be removed and be cast into the sea,' and does not doubt in his heart, but believes that those things he says will be done, he will have whatever he says.

24 Therefore I say to you, whatever things you ask when you pray, believe that you receive them, *and you will have* them.'"

God's words and our words are containers.

The Word of God contains the blood of God according to John chapter 6, and our words of sin spoken to God carry our old sin nature into Jesus. We saw how God's word can now bring us back into a union and oneness with God the Creator.

We need to meditate upon and study the Blood Covenant with God, which will then take you through the "Veil" into His presence. This is really needed when we are in some sort of affliction.

Hear and speak.

We not only need to hear the Word from God, but then we need to speak it out loud so that we hear it, God hears it, angels hear it, and the satanic forces hear it. The Word received and then spoken will be like the security force at airports. It will stop the evil thoughts at the TSA screening machine, and only allow God's thoughts to prevail. As God's thoughts prevail we will be encouraged to walk the overcoming lifestyle and not give up during our dark times.

You will not submit to the enemy's goal of giving up hope and thus speaking the words that the enemy has designed for you to speak.

The discipline of the tongue is important. It is important to remember that most of the time your tongue will only speak what is in your heart. Keep a guard on your heart and your tongue. Misusing the tongue is something that began with Adam. However, we are called to turn that around by hearing what God says, and then speaking it to dominate the earth as God originally intended. Remember, Jesus made you a king. Kings rule by their commands expressed by their words.

Matthew 12:36 says,

36 "But I say to you that for every idle word men may speak, they will give account of it in the day of judgment."

Complaining can block your fruit bearing and keep you from the "Promise Land."

To complain about anything is very dangerous, with one exception. That exception is when we need to pour out our hearts to God and let Him know about all of our sin. Make sure, however, that you frame your conversation with God about your complaints as a confession of sin, something that you are confessing that you do not like. To actually issue a complaint to God is what I am calling dangerous. It is also dangerous to complain to others. I know it may be a difficult habit to stop and I understand that not everybody is at the point of accepting everything in their lives as something that God wants them to work through. My advice is to work to stop complaining by learning to trust God at a deeper level.

Jesus did not complain.

Hebrews 12:2 b (Amplified Bible) says,

2 "...He, for the joy [of obtaining the prize] that was set before Him, endured the cross, despising and ignoring the shame, and is now seated at the right hand of the throne of God."

Abraham.

It is amazing that after all that Abraham (Abram) had been through that he did not complain when God told him to sacrifice Isaac.

Genesis 22:1-3 says,

1 "Now it came to pass after these things that God tested Abraham, and said to him, "Abraham!" And he said, "Here I am."

2 Then He said, "Take now your son, your only son Isaac, whom you love, and go to the land of Moriah, and offer him there as a burnt offering on one of the mountains of which I shall tell you."

3 So Abraham rose early in the morning and saddled his donkey, and took two of his young men with him, and Isaac his son; and he split the wood for the burnt offering, and arose and went to the place of which God had told him."

Old Testament Joseph.

Old Testament Joseph never complained even through the pit, through Potiphar's house, through the prison and through all the betrayals, the testimony was always, "The Lord was with him." The result was that Joseph's overcoming bore much fruit for the Kingdom of God. He fed the nations and saved Israel.

Israel in the Wilderness.

Numbers 14:27 says,

27 "How long shall I bear with this evil congregation who complain against Me? I have heard the complaints which the children of Israel make against Me."

God had promised the Promise Land (the land of fruit bearing) to those Israelites who He had supernaturally led out of Egypt. However, they did not enter into the promise due to their complaining.

Moses in the Wilderness.

Even Moses did not enter into the Promise Land, the land of fruit bearing, because of his complaining. He did not "hallow"

God. In other words, Moses did not properly represent God to the people. God wanted to give them mercy, but Moses, as a representative of God, called them "rebels," and made them think wrongfully of God.

Numbers 20:10-12 says,

10 "And Moses and Aaron gathered the assembly together before the rock; and he said to them, 'Hear now, you rebels! Must we bring water for you out of this rock?'

11 Then Moses lifted his hand and struck the rock twice with his rod; and water came out abundantly, and the congregation and their animals drank.

12 Then the LORD spoke to Moses and Aaron, 'Because you did not believe Me, to hallow Me in the eyes of the children of Israel, therefore you shall not bring this assembly into the land which I have given them.'"

Be sensitive and ask God to show you anything in your life that might block you from bearing fruit for His glory, especially complaining. Just this week before modifying this chapter, God convicted me of such a sin, and in repenting and receiving forgiveness I can move on as a fruit bearer to His glory, shining His light to a lost world.

I love the verse in the old Gospel hymn that says, "And the toils of the road will seem nothing when I get to the end of the way."

God's original blood relationship still creates a craving, a longing inside of us for the blood covenant with God.

In spite of the fact that Adam became disconnected with God, he and his descendants maintained a deep craving for that original connection. I believe that craving has been passed down through the generations in much the same way that Adam's sin has been passed down.

I believe that in each of us exists a craving for that blood connection that Adam once had. I believe that the more primitive and even Eastern cultures, which rely more upon their intuition than their intellect, sense that craving for the blood covenant in a greater way. God's purpose is to continually change us into "children," so that we may sense that craving.

One of the ways to develop and enhance this craving is to practice a valuable exercise of 'taking up your cross" on a daily basis, that means, to exchange God's will for your will, God's thoughts for your thoughts, and God's emotions for your emotions. One way to help you with this is given in our publication The Flowing River, which may be found at our web site, http://www.isob-bible.org/flowingriver.htm.

The power of your decision.

The power created in your life by making a decision is extraordinary! Something very powerful happens in the spiritual realm each time you make a final decision about a matter. If you will make a daily decision, as mentioned in Romans 12:1-2, to offer yourself as a living sacrifice, you will see God's Word open to you in a brand new way. If you will make a daily decision to govern your words by Scripture and not by your feelings, you will see blessings come that you never expected. You will have a new sense of God's presence and His nearness. Scripture references include John 14:21-23, which says that God makes Himself real to those who obey His words.

Speaking God's Word will bring His Kingdom back to earth.

Now we mere humans have the privilege of partnership to bring God's Kingdom to this earth. As we fellowship with Jesus through the Holy Spirit and with the Father, He speaks His Word, His will into our hearts. That Word is a rhema, or a customized Word for us individually, which is meant to bring fruit that will supply our needs, change our character and glorify God through us for the building of His Kingdom.

My personal experience with this process since 1979 is interesting. While I do not have room here for all of my testimonies, I can say that God has always done according to the following Scripture.

Ephesians 3:20 (Amplified Bible) says,

20 "Now to Him Who, by (in consequence of) the [action of His] power that is at work within us, is able to [carry out His purpose and] do superabundantly, far over and above all that we [dare] ask or think [infinitely beyond our highest prayers, desires, thoughts, hopes, or dreams]."

Our ideas, dreams and visions for our lives are invariably too small for God, or at best they miss the mark. However, this I know, not only through the Word but also by personal experience. That is, if you will simply take the rhema that God gives you and speak it out on a regular basis, He will do an "Ephesians 3:20 job" with you. Speaking in tongues for long periods of time will also accomplish the same purpose. Speak God's Words of life and you will reverse the curse that Adam brought in!

Chapter 3
Grace by Inheritance.

In the previous chapter we wrote about the great Divine plan to answer man's rebellion (sin). God did not accept the religious answer that Adam and Eve attempted to provide to their new condition of separation from the life of God. They acted out their new fallen nature in shame, blame, and religion. God provided His plan, a new blood covenant, the blood transfer from Himself to his fallen creature in order to secure and re-institute oneness and inter-union of natures, by blood.

We as humans often feel that our life began when we were born. Wrong! When we were born we had already inherited our nature. We had inherited natural things, like personality, disposition, hair color, eye color, appearances, etc. We also had inherited spiritual things like blessings and curses. Therefore, our life really began with an inheritance about which we had absolutely no choice. So much of our destiny in life existed before we did.

We inherited grace with God.

What is grace? Grace with God simply means that God provides His Holy Spirit in you, the New Creation race, so that He may perform those things and provide those things for you and through you that your old Adamic nature could not have provided or performed. Grace is simply Jesus living His life in you through the Holy Spirit. It is the means to return you to "normal."

Normal is being a blood child of the Creator God in a deep personal relationship with Him. Normal is being a co-laborer with Him in bringing the Kingdom of God to this earth.

Grace by inheritance means that the provision of this grace was simply something that we obtained by inheritance, not by any works or qualifications of our own. The Law makes demands, but Grace supplies the power.

However unlike the natural nature that we inherited from our earthly parents which was given to us without our power to receive or reject, God's inheritance requires us to receive or reject it.

The grace, or free gift, of being connected to our Creator by blood covenant existed in eternity. It was God's original plan!

When did God accomplish the blood covenant transfer? God had the solution accomplished even before the problem occurred.

Revelation 13:8b says,

8 "..the Lamb slain from the foundation of the world."

1 Corinthians 2:7-8 says,

7 "But we speak the wisdom of God in a mystery, the hidden wisdom which God ordained before the ages for our glory,

8 which none of the rulers of this age knew; for had they known, they would not have crucified the Lord of glory."

In a way the rulers of this age had no choice. Although God did not violate their free choice in crucifying Jesus, what they carried out was ordained and ordered before the angels; demons and Satan were ever created. They thought they had control but they were really puppets in the hand of a mighty God!

God is always ahead of Satan and ahead of us. In God's mind, in the files of eternal history, Jesus had already taken Adam's place as the one disconnected from God. That is why God covered Adam and Eve with coats of a slain animal, with blood. The blood represented the blood covenant, which reconnects disconnected man with God.

What does *everlasting* mean?

Hebrews 13:20 says,

20 "Now may the God of peace who brought up our Lord Jesus from the dead, that great Shepherd of the sheep, through the blood of the everlasting [aioniov] *covenant."*

The word *everlasting* (*aioniov*) does not mean that it will last now and forever. It means eternal, which is without beginning or end, something that always existed, outside of time.

Allow me to use my imagination a bit to help us see this idea. I do admit that it is impossible for a time creature to describe what goes on in eternity, but this is as close as I can get.

Back before time, Satan rebelled and took one third of the angels with him. God may have had a conference within the Trinity that went like this:

"My beloved let Us talk. Lucifer has rebelled and has taken on evil. He has attracted many angels to join his rebellion. You all know that we have plans to create a race called Adam, or man, from the dust of a planet we are going to create called Earth. Spirit, you will dwell inside of man. Man will have a free volition (will), however, to choose to be part of us. We will do all we can to attract man with our love.

However, man will be vulnerable to Satan. Satan is going to tempt Adam to rebel and Adam will go for it. Therefore, we need to also create a second race of people even before we create Adam. We will call this second race, the New Creation. Son, this is going to cost you all. Are you willing?"

"Father, I understand that this new race will, by requirement, need to be connected by a blood covenant, that I Myself will need to become a man and dwell on Earth. I understand that I must walk the trench of blood shed on behalf of Adam and Adam's descendants because the Adam race is not able to keep the covenant with Us. Father, I understand that this must, by necessity, be My blood. Father, I will do that."

"Son, I therefore declare you crucified before the foundation of the world. You must suffer much. I am sorry, but there is no other way. You know that in order to fulfill everything for this New Creation race, I must also forsake You, turn My back on You"

"Father, that will be more pain than any being will ever suffer, but because of our love Father, let it be."

I needed to express the above conversation in terms of a time-oriented person. However, we should know that God is not restricted by time. Some people say that God does "know things before they happen." But it is not a completely true statement; it is a statement from a perspective of a time-restricted being. The word *before* would infer time. But God exists outside of time; He experiences the past, present and future simultaneously!

Therefore two races existed when Adam was created, Adam and the New Creation. Remember, Jesus is called the Last Adam.

We need to comprehend that God knows our future before it happens. He knows the end from the beginning. It is a fearful thing to be in union with such a Being!

Romans 5:20 has an interesting insight into this idea.

Romans 5:20 says,

> *20 "Moreover the law entered that the offense might abound. But where sin abounded, grace abounded much more."*

The first word "abounded" means to strike like an arrow, but the next word "abounded" means that grace was there ahead of time.

In your life, when sin strikes you, when challenges seem to overwhelm you, remember, God's grace was there ahead of time. His grace is there to catch you, to turn the evil into a blessing!

Isaiah 65:24 says,

> *24 "It shall come to pass that before they call, I will answer; and while they are still speaking, I will hear."*

It is again stated in Hebrews 9:14 that our blood covenant existed before man was created.

Hebrews 9:14 says,

> *14 "How much more shall the blood of Christ, who through the eternal Spirit offered Himself without spot*

to God, cleanse your conscience from dead works to serve the living God?"

Our new blood union established through the blood of the everlasting covenant, the eternal covenant with the I AM, the Eternal Being. It is a gift that has an incalculable value!

It can be difficult to believe that you have inherited the nature of the I AM, the Creator God! Most Christians struggle with this amazing fact. They just cannot believe the truth, that we really do have His nature in us, that we are really reborn creatures through the blood covenant. What is even more difficult to understand is that the I AM became one of us, a limited-time being (Philippians 2:8).

My opinion is that all men have been given this inheritance, this new birth. Unfortunately, God has to erase many of the names before time ends.

"Grace by inheritance" can be expressed by comparing your natural birth by your natural parents. If you received great intelligence, or excellent health, or perhaps a financial inheritance, that is considered grace. You actually had nothing to do with it. It was inherited from the progenitor of your race. You did not earn it, nor did you work for it. On the other hand, if you inherited some curse from your natural parents, in the same way that did not come to you by your own efforts or sin. However, you now have a new progenitor, a new inheritance. How? You have been given a blood covenant as an inheritance to accept or refuse.

God the Father is now the progenitor of a new race, a resurrected race.

What does "Father" really mean? W.E. Vine Bible Dictionary defines the Greek word "Father" as "Pater," from a root signifying a nourisher, protector, upholder, the nearest ancestor, the progenitor of the race of people; the originator of a family or company of persons animated by the same spirit as himself. Regeneration is from two words: "palin" means again, and "genesis" means birth. Palingenis or regeneration is actually changing who your Father is.

W.E. Vine Bible Dictionary also defines the word "Abba" as an Aramaic word used by infants to call their daddy. It betokens unreasoning trust, while "Father" or "Pater" expresses an intelligent apprehension of the relationship. The two together express the love and intelligent confidence of the child.

When the new birth happened in your life, your progenitor changed from Adam to God. Therefore you inherit all things from Him. That is grace!

Titus 3:5 says,

> *5 "not by works of righteousness which we have done, but according to His mercy He saved us, through the washing of regeneration and renewing of the Holy Spirit."*

It is about relationship with our new Father.

Now it is your choice. You have the possibility of a great inheritance, a great gift of and by grace, which you could not earn, nor do you deserve. However, you must respond in a covenant way! This is where too many people miss it. Not only do you need to respond in a blood covenant way, you must also engage in spiritual warfare against the demons under Satan whose goal is to steal your inheritance.

The Father God so coveted to be in relationship with us that He went to almost unbelievable means to achieve it. Now it is our choice to enter into that relationship and do our part to keep it right. That includes spiritual warfare because the demonic forces will do all they can to prevent the relationship between you and God.

We may have an inheritance legally, but we must fight for it experientially, at least in order to experience it during this lifetime.

2 Corinthians 10:4-5 says,

"4 For the weapons of our warfare are not carnal but mighty in God for pulling down strongholds,
5 casting down arguments and every high thing that exalts itself against the knowledge of God, bringing every thought into captivity to the obedience of Christ,"

Joshua experienced this -Joshua 1:2-3, 5 says,

2 "Moses My servant is dead. Now therefore, arise, go over this Jordan, you and all this people, to the land which I am giving to them – the children of Israel.
3 Every place that the sole of your foot will tread upon I have given you, as I said to Moses."
5 "No man shall be able to stand before you all the days of your life; as I was with Moses, so I will be with you. I will not leave you nor forsake you."

Notice what God told Joshua. First, He said I am giving, and then, He said I have given. It was a done deal, past tense. God had given them the Promise Land. But then He added two things. First, He told Joshua that his foot would have to tread upon the land, and next, He inferred to Joshua that there would be warfare in order to actually posses the promised inheritance.

Romans 8:16-17 states that we indeed are children who are joint heirs with Christ. We are heirs and therefore we have an inheritance coming. However in this passage of Scripture it is clear that we are only joint heirs if we *suffer* with Him. I submit that it means what it meant to Joshua, warfare.

Romans 8:16-17 says,

16 "The Spirit Himself bears witness with our spirit that we are children of God,
17 and if children, then heirs – heirs of God and joint heirs with Christ, if indeed we suffer with Him, that we may also be glorified together."

The word *suffer* means to feel pain, to experience troubles and persecution.

Grace applied to Jacob.

In Genesis chapter 32 Jacob knew he had to confront his brother Esau who, according to history, had a determination to kill Jacob (Genesis 27:41). In this chapter it tells how Jacob attempted to bribe Esau with a huge financial gift consisting of many possessions.

However, as told in Genesis 32:24-32, Jacob had an encounter with God. Jacob wrestled with God until daybreak, and would not release Him until he received a blessing. The blessing came in the form of God touching Jacob's thigh, the strongest part of human flesh. That touch put Jacob's thigh out of joint for the rest of his life. This is where God renamed Jacob to Israel, from "deceiver" to "God prevails."

This is a picture of God's great desire to bless us by "breaking our flesh," or our old Adamic nature, so that He may prevail in our lives. If grace is God living in us, then often times grace is increased by our old nature being decreased. We need more of Him and less of us.

Next time you experience a "breaking" in your life, give praise to God like Jacob did, do not let go of Him not matter what, and you will experience an increased presence of God in your life manifested to others.

It is interesting to note that when Jacob, now Israel, really did encounter Esau as told in Genesis chapter 33, that Esau did not want Jacob's bribes, but rather expressed a great love for him. Do you suppose that that change in Esau's attitude towards Jacob had to do something with God's grace being so manifested in Jacob that Esau was overcome by the presence of God? I do.

One major motivation for God to give you grace is that He wants to have close fellowship with you.

He wants His love and your love to find expression with one another. This is an "ache" in the heart of our Father God. Without grace, God could not express His love for you nor could you express your love for Him.

Love Satisfied!

Ephesians 2:4 (Amplified Bible) expresses it well,

4 But God – so rich is He in His mercy! Because of ***and in order to satisfy the great and wonderful and intense love with which He loved us,***

Now, you need to respond to the blood covenant by pursuing a relationship with Jesus. That personal living touch with Jesus is the only way you will prevail in warfare and experience the inheritance.

God is not asking you, by your own will, to overcome the challenges in life, but He is inviting you to discipline your life, to relate to Him and get to know Him. His power will work if you do. That is grace! However, you must receive the grace by exercising relationship disciplines with God. You are already connected with Him. Legally you already have your inheritance, but experientially you must realize that through being in vital and authentic contact with God. Exercising your relationship with Him will bring the actual realization of your inheritance to you.

Relationship Skills and Disciplines.

God is inviting you to discipline your life to relate to Him and get to know Him. This is how the blood covenant blessings flow into your life:

1. **Make a firm decision to pursue the relationship.** Offer yourself completely to God (Romans 12:1-2). This is our blood covenant response to a mighty blood covenant offered to us by God.

2. **Take time to listen.** You must take in His Word. Words are blood covenant containers. You must always be in a disciplined Bible study of some kind. Ask the Holy Spirit to show you.

3. **Take time to talk**: Speak your words. Some people write down their thoughts and feelings in a journal, which can be very valuable. Be gut level honest. Honesty with your blood covenant

partner Jesus will cause your sin to go on Him. You cannot and will not overcome any bondage without this gut level honesty.

4. Take time to talk. Speak His Words. Read Psalms and Proverbs by the day. One discipline is to read aloud five Psalms every morning. Use the system of the calendar. As an example, on the 24th of the month read Psalms 24, 54, 84, 114 and 144. Also read Proverb 24. In this system the student will read all Psalms and Proverbs every month. Using this system renews the mind, speaks the Word to Satan, and allows the suffering believer to relate his/her emotions to the Psalmist's. Provisions can be made for months with 31 days, and for Psalm 119. God may lead you to other Scriptures to read out loud as you progress, but this is a good start, and can be a continued blessing for the rest of your life.

5. Obey God. Ask God to give you something simple, something small every day that you may obey. It may be just encouraging another. It may be not driving down the same street that fed your addiction. It may be confessing your sin to Him.

This is a big thing!

John 14:21-23 says that when we obey His Word that He will reveal more and more of Himself to us. Once you have "seen" Jesus, your relationship with Him will no longer be a discipline, but it will be a passionate pursuit. The apostle Paul had this passion.

Philippians 3:10 (Amplified Bible) says,

> *10 "[For my determined purpose is] that I may know Him [that I may progressively become more deeply and intimately acquainted with Him, perceiving and recognizing and understanding the wonders of His Person more strongly and more clearly], and that I may in that same way come to know the power outflowing from His resurrection [which it exerts over believers], and that I may so share His sufferings as to be continually transformed [in spirit into His likeness even] to His death, [in the hope]."*

6. Communion. Take communion on a regular basis. Many people take it daily.

7. Stay in fellowship. It is important to be in fellowship with strong Bible believing, Spirit filled believers, for refreshing and encouragement.

Chapter 4
More About Blood Covenants

Life, real life, is in the blood.

Leviticus 17:11 says,

11 "For the life of the flesh is *in the blood, and I have given it to you upon the altar to make atonement for your souls; for it is the blood that makes atonement for the soul."*

Western thinking compared to Eastern, Oriental, Hebrew thinking.

Henry Clay Trumbull, for most of his life, researched blood covenants in ancient cultures, including Bible cultures. In his book, The Blood Covenant [2], he states:

From the beginning, and everywhere, blood seems to have been looked upon as pre-eminently the representative of life; as indeed, in a peculiar sense, life itself. The transference of blood from one organism to another has been counted the transference of life, with all that life includes. The inter-commingling of blood by its inter-transference has been understood as equivalent to an inter-commingling of natures. Two natures inter-commingled, by the inter-commingling of blood, have been considered as forming, thenceforward, one blood, one life, one nature, one soul – in two organisms. The inter-commingling of natures by the inter-commingling of blood has been deemed possible between man and a lower organism, - even between man and Deity, actually or by symbol; - as well as between man and his immediate fellow.

Blood, as life, has been looked upon as belonging, in the highest sense, to the Author of all life. The taking of life has been seen to be the prerogative of its Author; ...

---

[2] Trumbull, H. Clay, *The Blood Covenant,* Impact Books Inc. Kirkwood, MO, 1975, pages 202-204.

The heart of any living organism, as the blood-source and the blood – fountain, has been recognized as the representative of its owner's highest personality, and as the diffuser of the issues of his life and nature.

A covenant of blood, a covenant made by the inter-commingling of blood, has been recognized as the closest, the holiest, and the most indissoluble, compact conceivable. Such a covenant clearly involves an absolute surrender of one's separate self, and an irrevocable merging of one's individual nature into the dual, or the multiplied, personality included in the compact. Man's highest and noblest outreachings of soul have, therefore, been for such a union with the divine nature as is typified in this human covenant of blood.

A blood covenant demands unwavering loyalty. To waiver is to die. That is one reason I believe that so many civilized Western minded thinkers have a difficult time with their relationship with God. They don't understand the absoluteness of the relationship. Many Eastern thinking Christians don't have access to good solid Bible teaching, but when they find out about the blood, they latch on to the idea with all they have.

One who breaks the covenant does it to his/her own death. Jeremiah 34:17-20 says,

17 "Therefore thus says the LORD: 'You have not obeyed Me in proclaiming liberty, every one to his brother and every one to his neighbor. Behold, I proclaim liberty to you,' says the LORD – 'to the sword, to pestilence, and to famine! And I will deliver you to trouble among all the kingdoms of the earth.

18 And I will give the men who have transgressed My covenant, who have not performed the words of the covenant which they made before Me, when they cut the calf in two and passed between the parts of it–

19 the princes of Judah, the princes of Jerusalem, the eunuchs, the priests, and all the people of the land who passed between the parts of the calf –

20 I will give them into the hand of their enemies and into the hand of those who seek their life. Their dead bodies shall be for meat for the birds of the heaven and the beasts of the earth.'"

What happens when you do not keep the covenant perfectly? God knew this would happen; therefore He walked the blood covenant ditch on behalf of man. In a later chapter we will cover the details of this from Genesis chapter 15. We will see that Abram did not walk the bloody covenant ditch, but he saw two forms of Deity in the covenant ditch. I believe that one was Jesus and the other was the Father, or perhaps the Holy Spirit. Jesus took the death of you, the covenant breaker! Then He was raised from the dead having left the Old Creation in Hell. He was raised as a New Creation, the first born of the new race.

Galatians 3:13-14 says,

13 "Christ has redeemed us from the curse of the law, having become a curse for us (for it is written, "Cursed is everyone who hangs on a tree"),

14 that the blessing of Abraham might come upon the Gentiles in Christ Jesus, that we might receive the promise of the Spirit through faith."

God cannot lie! He swore to death that He would keep that covenant, knowing that Abram and you and I would not keep it. Thus, He died for *our* infidelity to the covenant. What a deal!

Hebrews 6:17-18 says,

17 "Thus God, determining to show more abundantly to the heirs of promise the immutability of His counsel, confirmed it by an oath,

18 that by two immutable things, in which it is impossible for God to lie, we might have strong consolation, who have fled for refuge to lay hold of the hope set before us."

Titus 1:2 says,

2 "In hope of eternal life which God, who cannot lie, promised before time began."

What is a friend?

The word "friend" in the Oriental/Hebrew culture means a blood covenant partner.

Proverbs 18:24 (KJV) says,

24 "A man that hath friends must shew himself friendly: and there is a friend that sticketh closer than a brother."

Many cultures that still appreciate blood covenants have a saying, "Blood is thicker than water." The water they refer to is the birth water of the mother, indicating that blood covenant friends are more closely related than children of the same mother. Another way they say it is, "Blood is thicker than milk."

"Friend" is covenant language. It means the most intimate, loyal and strongest inter-union between two beings. When Jesus called Judas "friend" in the Garden of Gethsemane, He was indicting him of breaking the blood covenant. Matthew 26:50.

John 15:15 (KJV) says,

15 "Henceforth I call you not servants; for the servant knoweth not what his lord doeth: but I have called you friends; for all things that I have heard of my Father I have made known unto you."

The first 8 verses of John 15 tells about bearing fruit, which includes supplying our needs, if we appreciate and appropriate the blood covenant.

Kissing is a blood covenant act. Jesus called Judas "friend." When one kisses he/she can only kiss one person and that speaks of exclusivity or covenant. When one kisses on the lips, then it is codified as a two-way exclusive relationship. Be careful whom you kiss. Many godly people feel that it is wrong to kiss *anyone* on the mouth that is not your spouse, not even your children.

The word remembrance is a very powerful word.
Luke 22:19 says,

> *19 "And He took bread, gave thanks and broke it, and gave it to them, saying, 'This is My body which is given for you; do this in remembrance of Me.'"*

Vines Complete Expository Dictionary defines the word *remembrance* as follows: "it denotes an unassisted recalling, a remembrance prompted by another, however in classical Greek the words are easily interchangeable. This denotes His presence, not in memory of, but in affectionate calling of the Person Himself to mind; an awakening of the mind to the sacrifices under the Law [the blood]."

A new vision for taking communion.

In the taking of communion we are to picture and remember in our mind, in our imagination, Jesus walking the blood covenant trench on behalf of Abraham and us. We are to picture Jesus on the Cross taking the stripes and torture and bleeding for us. We are to remember His blood. We are to remember to take up our cross, to offer ourselves to Him as a living sacrifice. And finally we are to remember who we are in the resurrection power and New Birth.

Remember who you are. It is all about your identity.

Remember what He did in the blood covenant.

Remember who you are in the blood covenant.

Remember how your life may not measure up to His character.

Remember that when you repent and confess, His power will heal you and do what is needed.

John 15:16 says,

"16 "You did not choose Me, but I chose you and appointed ***[laid you flat, horizontal and helpless]*** *you that you should go*

and bear fruit, and that your fruit should remain, that whatever you ask the Father in My name He may give you."

If we truly meditate upon the Word of God as it applies to the blood covenant, we will eventually know who we are in fact and in truth! Most faith and behavior issues with Christians stem from the fact that they have never really believed in their hearts who God has made them to be through the blood covenant.

My wife has always said to our children, even our adult children, as they went out the door, "Remember who you are!"

As I was taking communion recently, the Lord said to me, "Larry, as you take this remember who *you* are." This was a reminder to me that the elements of the covenant are to remind us of the wonderful work that was done in order to regenerate us from sinners to New Creation beings. It is to remind us that we have been crucified with Christ, and have already been raised from the dead in Him. We are also to "remember" who we are in the spiritual sense.

In 1 Corinthians 11 Paul gives a warning that many believers are suffering needlessly and even dying at an early age because of taking communion unworthily.

1 Corinthians 11:29-31 (Amplified Bible) says,

> *29 "For anyone who eats and drinks without discriminating and recognizing with due appreciation that [it is Christ's] body, eats and drinks a sentence (a verdict of judgment) upon himself.*
>
> *30 That [careless and unworthy participation] is the reason many of you are weak and sickly, and quite enough of you have fallen into the sleep of death.*
>
> *31 For if we searchingly examined ourselves [detecting our shortcomings and recognizing our own condition], we should not be judged and penalty decreed [by the divine judgment]."*

I am going to share this idea of "Christ's body" in two aspects.

1. The universal Body of Christ, the body of believers in the world.

It is dangerous to be loose or double minded about God's blood covenant family. Paul had admonished these people for at least three things: 1) being in disunity, 2) harboring an ungodly behavior prior to taking the communion, and 3) for "not rightly discerning" or, as it says in the Amplified Bible, "without discriminating and recognizing with due appreciation that [it is Christ's] body." I have seen men of God suffer needlessly because they treated the earthly Body of Christ in a disrespectful way.

2. Your body as Christ's possession.

You know that you are the temple of the Holy Spirit. Your body is not yours but Christ's. When you put harmful substances into your body, you are not recognizing with due appreciation that it is Christ's body, and you are putting judgment on yourself. Imagine if you were looking at the Temple of God in front of you. You see white fire and smoke with loud noises coming forth from the Holy of Holies. Can you imagine yourself walking up to this Temple and writing graffiti on its walls with a paintbrush?

We should not be presumptuous with our bodies. When we take in harmful substances we should not wonder why God does not heal us.

God is Holy! If you wish to partake in the benefits of the covenant then be holy, be like He is! Treat His earthly Body properly. Don't criticize and gossip. Don't talk negatively, don't harbor ungodly thoughts rather take them to the Cross. Submit to your proper authorities, tithe, give to the poor, be unselfish, love your enemies, live a life of love, and don't judge others. When you don't live up to the pattern, then judge yourself, confess your sin, and Jesus will cleanse you. Be very prayerful about what you put into your body. If you want to change, ask Jesus to baptize you in His Holy Spirit and fire!

Remember who God is. Jesus made it clear that we partake of the covenant by His Words. Read this Scripture again and let it soak in.

John 6:53-56; 63 says,

53 "Then Jesus said to them, 'Most assuredly, I say to you, unless you eat the flesh of the Son of Man and drink His blood, you have no life in you.
54 Whoever eats My flesh and drinks My blood has eternal life, and I will raise him up at the last day.
55 For My flesh is food indeed, and My blood is drink indeed.
56 He who eats My flesh and drinks My blood abides in Me, and I in him.'"
63 "It is the Spirit who gives life; the flesh profits nothing. The words that I speak to you are spirit, and they *are life."*

Trust God's Word, it is His covenant transfer agent to you. Heaven and earth may pass away but His Word will stand forever! The reason many Christians cannot trust God's Word is that they cannot trust their own words. They are by nature disloyal people and liars. If that is you, don't fret, just get honest and repent. God will honor your honesty and repentance.

What if your experiences seem to challenge your blood covenant with God?

Are we guaranteed a problem free life? For sure no! He will make us overcomers, in His definition of that word. He is not only preparing us for Heaven but He is also defeating His enemies on this earth, and planting His Kingdom here.

Through the blood covenant God took your Adamic sinful nature into Himself and took it to the Cross for all the punishment due to you. That gives you protection from going to Hell for eternity, and also is valuable for operating your life here on earth.

Through the blood covenant God put His divine nature into you through the Holy Spirit. It is part of God's eternal goal to develop the Kingdom of God on this earth. That will include spiritual warfare of many types.

Please remember that Jesus did not "destroy" Satan when He spoke the Word to Him as in Luke 4:12. Satan just departed for a while. However Jesus' real victory over Satan was gained by spiritual ambush. He allowed an unrighteous group of people who were motivated by unrighteous Satan, to crucify Him. That is what legally defeated Satan. Now Jesus is looking to us to defeat the various demonic forces in our realm here on earth through the same tactic, ambush.

Perhaps the suffering you are experiencing is not being caused by your neglect or sin, but is just being allowed for the ambush of some principalities and powers here on earth. Hang on!!

His ways are so much higher than our ways.

Just think; the Blood Covenant has returned us to "normal," it has saved us from eternity in Hell, and guaranteed us eternity in Heaven. However we live in a sin-infested world and in intense spiritual warfare. God's ways in this life often will be revealed to us, but sometimes He keeps His ways to Himself for at least for a while. Just ask Job and many others when you see them.

Isaiah 55:8-13 says,

"8 "For My thoughts are not your thoughts, Nor are your ways My ways," says the LORD.

9 "For as the heavens are higher than the earth, So are My ways higher than your ways, And My thoughts than your thoughts.

10 "For as the rain comes down, and the snow from heaven, And do not return there, But water the earth, And make it bring forth and bud, That it may give seed to the sower And bread to the eater,

*11 So shall My word be that goes forth from My mouth; It shall not return to Me void, But it shall accomplish **what I please**, And it shall prosper in the thing **for which I sent it.***

12 "For you shall go out with joy, And be led out with peace; The mountains and the hills Shall break forth into singing before you, And all the trees of the field shall clap their hands.

13 Instead of the thorn shall come up the cypress tree, And instead of the brier shall come up the myrtle tree; And it shall be to the LORD for a name, For an everlasting sign that shall not be cut off."

His peace and His joy will come through our intimacy with Him, and someday we will understand!

Some stories.

David Livingstone

[3] David Livingstone, historically one of the great missionaries of modern times, in the middle 1800s determined to reach the Africans with the Gospel. On one of his efforts to go into the interior he was advised that the only way to do so would be to make a covenant with one of the chiefs. The deal was that the chief would give Livingstone his old staff with wire wrapped all around it in trade for Livingstone's goat. Livingstone needed the goat for milk, to settle his ulcers, but his people convinced him to make the trade. They cut the covenant with blood. As David Livingstone then approached each interior tribe he would hold up the staff, and the entire tribe would bow and worship, knowing that Livingstone was in covenant with the strongest chief in the area. They understood that looking at Livingstone was the same as looking at the chief with whom he had cut covenant. What about you? Who does Satan see when he looks at you?

Malcolm Smith

Malcolm Smith tells the story of a journey into an African village. On the way he stopped at a bank to exchange funds. The teller put her fingers over the counter waiting for Mr. Smith to reciprocate. After asking his guides, he discovered that this represented two people exchanging blood at the tips of their fingers to insure that no dishonesty would take place in the transaction.

---

[3] David Livingstone http://home.vicnet.net.au/~neils/africa/livingstone.htm

The next day, Mr. Smith met the village chief, a very primitive scarcely clad man. He told the chief that God had sent him with a message for his village. When the chief asked about the message, Mr. Smith put out his fingers in the blood covenant sign. The chief was totally overwhelmed and bowed down and accepted Jesus. He could barely conceive that the Creator would cut a blood covenant with him. The entire village was transformed.

Haiti

During our trips to Haiti we have heard many stories about the culture's view of blood and covenants. Over 200 years ago, Haiti was given to Satan by the blood of a pig ritual. Voodoo and the related religions all understand the value of blood in spiritual matters. One pastor told us the story of a Voodoo priest who came to him in order to better understand his religion. The pastor had been casting out demons, and this Voodoo priest wanted to know where the power came from. The priest told the pastor that his best friend had died recently and that even the blood of a chicken could not heal him. The pastor began to tell this man about the blood of Jesus. He was gloriously saved and is now serving in the church.

The Mafia

The Mafia does business with blood covenant relationships. If a Mafia member speaks against his brother, his life will be taken. That gives us some kind of a clue of how we should be speaking of our blood covenant brothers and sisters. I dare not speak a negative word against one, lest I am speaking against Jesus and will be judged!

Shaking hands is a blood covenant gesture. Originally blood was passed between the two parties in the grasp, each guaranteeing that the other would not be hurt.

Chapter 5
Cain and Abel

The first two children of Adam and Eve were named Cain and Abel. Abel raised sheep and Cain had a garden with fruit and vegetables. In my opinion, at that time God had not yet given permission for mankind to eat meat; that came after the flood with Noah. That being true, Abel must have been raising the sheep for clothing and offering only. This is what he had learned from his mom and dad. The relationship between Cain and Abel should have been one of trading altar animals for vegetables to eat, but apparently Cain felt that he did not need a blood covenant offering.

Genesis 4:1-4 says,

1 "Now Adam knew Eve his wife, and she conceived and bore Cain, and said, 'I have acquired a man from the LORD.'

2 Then she bore again, this time his brother Abel. Now Abel was a keeper of sheep, but Cain was a tiller of the ground.

3 And in the process of time it came to pass that Cain brought an offering of the fruit of the ground to the LORD.

4 Abel also brought of the firstborn of his flock and of their fat. And the LORD respected Abel and his offering,"

The Lord God accepted Abel's animal offering and the blood that was shed. The Lord God did not accept Cain's fruit offering.

Adam and Eve taught both boys to bring an animal offering to God for their sin so that they could be connected to God and be blood covenant friends with Him. It is interesting to note however that Eve's hope was in Abel and not Cain. Do you think that that it was a mother's intuition? Look what Eve said.

Genesis 4:25 says,

25 "And Adam knew his wife again, and she bore a son and named him Seth, 'For God has appointed another seed for me instead of Abel, whom Cain killed.'"

Religion verses blood covenant relationship.

Cain tried to please God with his fruit. God required a blood sacrifice. Abel brought his blood sacrifice. Cain was using "religion." Certainly, Cain had heard of the fig leaf attempt that did not work. The thing that really puzzles me is: How Cain could have actually heard God speak and in spite of that still attempted to placate this wonderful and fearful God with an offering from the fruit of the ground? The ground was cursed. Man did not need some kind of religious appeasement with God, he needed to be re-connected to His Spirit and that only by a complete exchange of character; man's for God's and God's for man's. God had to take on man's sinful nature and die with it. Only then could man possess his true identity. Life is in the blood!

The blood is a gift. Everything else is works.

Jesus' blood for our righteousness is a gift. Our works, even for the fruit of the ground, cannot bring us back into intimacy with God. The blood that Jesus shed on the Cross was sufficient to put us back into intimate touch with our Father God, Hebrews 9 and 10.

What a merciful God! God gave Cain an opportunity to repent.

Genesis 4:6-7 (Amplified Bible) says,

6 "And the Lord said to Cain, 'Why are you angry? And why do you look sad and depressed and dejected?

7 If you do well, will you not be accepted? And if you do not do well, sin crouches at your door; its desire is for you, but you must master it.'"

Notice what the Lord said to Cain about depression!

That word "master" means to take dominion over and rule.

How could he have taken dominion over sin? Cain could have taken dominion over the temptation to sin by taking his feelings and thoughts to the blood, or in our case, to the Cross. God gave Cain another chance to shed blood in respect of his need and in respect to the covenant, but Cain rejected the idea. Even when we act against God's character He gives us a chance to clear things up with Him. We cover this idea more at the end of this chapter.

Conscience compromised.

I submit that because Cain did not obey God that his conscience was compromised. I believe that is why he was able to kill his brother.

Genesis 4:8 says,

> *8 "Now Cain talked* (it means to strive and argue) *with Abel his brother; and it came to pass, when they were in the field, that Cain rose up against Abel his brother and killed him."*

I believe that much of what we see in human nature, without God and in the world today, is depicted in this event.

1. Jealousy and envy are the same as murder.

2. The other religions of this world hate those who depend upon Christ Jesus and His blood as the atonement for their sins.

3. This story shows how God is just and fair to give even potential murders the opportunity to come under His blood, grace and forgiveness.

4. Even some Christians who do not come to God in their honesty and ask for forgiveness have hatred towards other believers who do depend upon the blood.

What is the sentence or judgment for a murderer?

1 Corinthians 3:17 says,

> *17 "If anyone defiles the temple of God, God will destroy him. For the temple of God is holy, which* temple *you are."*

Cain's dilemma.

Look at Cain's dilemma. He could no longer be prosperous in agriculture, he could no longer enjoy God's presence, he would be a fugitive and a vagabond, a person who shakes with fear and wanders.

Genesis 4:9-15 says,

9 "Then the LORD said to Cain, 'Where is *Abel your brother?' He said, 'I do not know. Am I my brother's keeper?'*

10 And He said, 'What have you done? The voice of your brother's blood cries out to Me from the ground.

11 So now you are cursed from the earth, which has opened its mouth to receive your brother's blood from your hand.

12 When you till the ground, it shall no longer yield its strength to you. A fugitive and a vagabond you shall be on the earth.'

13 And Cain said to the LORD, 'My punishment is greater than I can bear!

14 Surely You have driven me out this day from the face of the ground; I shall be hidden from Your face; I shall be a fugitive and a vagabond on the earth, and it will happen that anyone who finds me will kill me.'

15 And the LORD said to him, 'Therefore, whoever kills Cain, vengeance shall be taken on him sevenfold.' And the LORD set a mark on Cain, lest anyone finding him should kill him."

The blood cursed and disabled the murderer's abilities. Notice, Cain's "ground" was cursed, the very venue that he used for murder. The blood of his victim disabled Cain's ability to carry out his mission and vocation in life. How much more does the blood of Jesus, which was poured out on Satan's ground, disable Satan?

Hebrews 12:24 says,

24 "To Jesus the Mediator of the new covenant, and to the blood of sprinkling that speaks better things than that *of Abel."*

Abel's blood spoke for vengeance, Jesus' blood speaks for mercy.

While Abel's blood spoke for vengeance on Cain, Jesus' blood speaks for mercy for all humans. However, Jesus' blood speaks for vengeance for His spiritual enemies, Satan and his whole crowd.

Our "blood" also speaks!

The blood of Jesus and even your blood defeats enemies.

However, our "blood," much again like Abel's, can also "speak" against Satan. Each time we "take up our cross," each time we forgive, refuse to blame, bless our enemies, refuse to engage in the things of this world, our "blood" speaks, curses and disables Satan's activities in our lives. It is so interesting that the very worst thing that our enemies can throw at us will actually give us victory!

This also applies to those the sufferings and challenges that affect our lives. We know that God is not the author of sufferings; however, He does have a law in place that is very valuable for us to know.

When someone "takes your blood, your life," it defeats the blood taker.

As you overcome that suffering or challenge, another group of demons and/or curses are defeated! What an awesome God we serve!

This is what I call the "Blood Law."

I believe that this law of the blood, even your "blood" defeating your enemies, was in existence before the universe was formed.

Revelation 13:8 b says,

> *8b "...the Book of Life of the Lamb slain from the foundation of the world."*

When Jesus took up His cross to shed His blood, it was the blood of His divine nature. When we take up our cross, the "blood" that we shed is the blood of the Adamic nature. However, they both defeat Satan and his demons.

How can we become an "Abel" and avoid being a "Cain?" How do we "bring the blood sacrifice" to God and not bring Him our "home grown vegetables?" By exercising our daily relationship skills. We take our thoughts captive (2 Corinthians 10:4) and bring them to Him, to His Cross. We bring our sin to the Cross, and we take up our cross by denying our fleshly desires and thoughts. We bring our ungodly desires and feelings to Him in honesty; we obey the Word. When we fail, we come back to Him and receive unmerited grace! This is the "blood life," the covenant life. Often in my life, I have seen immediate results. The black cloud lifts and His presence manifests. But even if I do not sense an immediate manifestation of His presence, I know my reward is on the way. 2 Corinthians 10:4-6 commands us to take our thoughts captive. I say that we should take our thoughts captive for the death penalty, and not for a life sentence!

Is there more than one way to commit a murder?

Hatred is murder according to Jesus.

The only way you can deal with hatred is to forgive the one you hate. Actually, if you even harbor resentment and unforgiveness you are in danger. This is why unforgiveness is so dangerous! When you speak against your blood covenant partner, (husband, wife, or other believer), you are a murderer.

Remember, the one who murders is the blood taker and he/she is the one who is cursed like Cain was. Hatred and unforgiveness will ruin your entire life.

Matthew 5:21-26 says,

> *21 "You have heard that it was said to those of old,* 'You shall not murder, *and whoever murders will be in danger of the judgment.'*
>
> *22 But I say to you that whoever is angry with his brother without a cause shall be in danger of the judgment. And whoever says to his brother, 'Raca!' shall be in danger of the council. But whoever says, 'You fool!' shall be in danger of hell fire.*

23 Therefore if you bring your gift to the altar, and there remember that your brother has something against you,

24 leave your gift there before the altar, and go your way. First be reconciled to your brother, and then come and offer your gift.

25 Agree with your adversary quickly, while you are on the way with him, lest your adversary deliver you to the judge, the judge hand you over to the officer, and you be thrown into prison.

26 Assuredly, I say to you, you will by no means get out of there till you have paid the last penny."

I suppose that there are simply two types of people.
1 John 3:10-12 says,

10 "In this the children of God and the children of the devil are manifest: Whoever does not practice righteousness is not of God, nor is he who does not love his brother.

11 For this is the message that you heard from the beginning, that we should love one another,

12 not as Cain who was of the wicked one and murdered his brother. And why did he murder him? Because his works were evil and his brother's righteous."

I believe that a person is either a murderer or a martyr. You will be one or the other, a martyr if you depend upon the blood, a murderer if you depend upon anything else!

What is a martyr? Jesus said, when asked of by His disciples when He would return, (my paraphrase), "That is not your business, but I am going to give you power through the Holy Spirit to be a martyr [witness]" (Acts 1:7-8). I believe that you are a martyr when you do not give up in the overcoming process, but press on. I believe that you are a martyr when you take up your cross and deny your flesh. I believe that you are a martyr when you won't shut upstop preaching with the Gospel no matter what the circumstances are, and even when you are falsely accused and persecuted.

Religion always kills. A blood covenant person always gives.
So many believers truly misunderstand God's love and His compassion for hurting people. Many become self-righteous, not on purpose, but by default, just by not staying tuned into God's Word and His presence and by not confessing their sins of judgment for others. If Jesus' blood covenant for us, on our behalf, made us children of God, people who are righteous with God, then how can we be self-righteous? Should we not rather be grateful for the gift?

When you trust in the blood, like Abel, you take on the character of the blood-giver, in this case God. If you do not trust in the blood, then you take on the character of Satan. It does not matter how much you read the Word or how often you go to church, or how many "do gooder" activities you are involved in. If you are not participating in the blood covenant relationship on blood covenant terms, you are by default a murderer!

If you are in a blood covenant relationship with God through Jesus, then it will progressively show in your habits of life. You will be desperately looking for a place to give. You will be unselfish. You will be hungry to find the hungry people and feed them. You will be searching for the hurting and poor people to comfort them, especially those who have hurt themselves. You will be helping those who religious people shun, like prostitutes, drug users, widows, orphans, and the down and outers, those who may not be a success in their culture. If you are practicing the blood covenant relationship with Jesus, you will have His character of loving the unlovable. You will fear judging others whose lives do not look like they are lining up with your standards or even God's standards.

Romans 13:8 says,

8 "Owe no one anything except to love one another, for he who loves another has fulfilled the law."

If you are practicing the blood covenant relationship with Jesus, you will not be concerned about your own financial welfare, you will know that if you give like your blood covenant Partner, Jesus, then He will take care of your finances through sowing and reaping.

2 Corinthians 9:6 says,

> *6 "But this I say: He who sows sparingly will also reap sparingly, and he who sows bountifully will also reap bountifully."*

If you are practicing the blood covenant relationship with Jesus, you will consider others better than yourself. Your level of pride will continually be decreasing and your humility will be increasing.

If you are practicing the blood covenant relationship with Jesus, you will be desperately looking for ways to submit to the proper authority.

You are a martyr when you take up your cross to live the love life, even if you do not lose your physical life.

Rejecting the covenant caused Cain to become a murderer. Cain's descendants created a culture of cities, music, businesses, perhaps politics, etc. God had to abandon that entire line and start over with Seth. The line of Seth led to Noah, through whom the righteous seed was carried forward. If Cain would have shed the animal's blood, a type of Christ's blood, and would have "taken up his cross," then vengeance would have been on Satan and not on himself.

Jesus did not shed His blood for the covenant only to keep you out of Hell. He wants you to inherit His character and be part of His Body.

The Lord made it simple. All we have to do is hold up the mirror of His character, walk in love and when we miss it be honest with Him about it and repent.

I don't know about you, but I am amazed that I am one of those who heard God speak and accepted His offer of the blood. I take no credit for it at all! There are billions of people living on this earth right now that totally reject the idea of a blood covenant with Deity. I do not understand their hearts! I suppose it looks too good to be true, or maybe someone has not shown them the real message. What is equally amazing are those "believers" who have in some way accepted the blood covenant sacrifice of Jesus, but who refuse to accept His character into their lives. How can that be? I think we all have room for improvement!

The only way we can inherit God's character is through His Word. We must hear Him speak and obey His authority. We must hear and obey like Abel and not like Cain, even if it "kills" us.

John 10:27 says,

27 "My sheep hear My voice, and I know them, and they follow Me."

What is it about Jesus saying that He desires us to hear His voice that is so complicated?

There have been false doctrines on both extremes about hearing God speak. I have heard the side of the "Scripture only" people stating that God has, once for all, spoken, and therefore He will speak no more. Poor people! I have heard the other side say that God speaks to them super-Scripturally, that is in their spirit without Scripture. Dangerous people! I have heard of a village in an Asian country that only had a few pages of Scripture, the part that said, "If thine eye offend thee, cut it out." They took this literally. I have had a personal experience with a renter in a property we owned who said, "God told me that you were to give me your house."

I heard Dr. Mark Rutland tell a story (what a story teller!) about meeting a minister on a flight from Los Angeles. This man was from a denomination that did not believe that God was currently speaking to His people, and he urged Dr. Rutland to express his opinion about this as a Pentecostal minister. Dr. Rutland simply asked this man, "Are you called to the ministry?" The man answered, "Yes." Then he asked, "Who called you?" The man turned his head to the window and did not speak a word for the rest of the flight.

My testimony.

In the case of hearing God speak, I do not believe in "balance" but in truth! Back in 1986 I heard a dear old brother in the Lord say that he was no longer a slave to sin. When I heard this I, coveted that experience. He had quoted Romans 6. I read Romans 6 over and over, and indeed it did say so.

Romans 6:11-12 says,

> *11 "Likewise you also, reckon yourselves to be dead indeed to sin, but alive to God in Christ Jesus our Lord.*
> *12 Therefore do not let sin reign in your mortal body, that you should obey it in its lust."*

Romans 6:6 says,

> *6 "Knowing this, that our old man was crucified with Him, that the body of sin might be done away with, that we should no longer be slaves of sin."*

Did I believe, in my mind, that I had been crucified with Christ? Yes! But did I really know it? No. I had not really heard the Lord *speak* this to me. The Lord spoke to me and told me to memorize that chapter and speak it out loud continually. I did. One day it became real to me. The *logos* (general Scripture) of the Word became *rhema* (a personalized Word from the Lord to me), and the resurrected Jesus spoke into my heart those Words. It burned into my soul and ever since then I have never doubted it.

Revelation knowledge (*rhema*).

Galatians 4:9 states that not only do we know God, but that we are also known by Him, i.e., He lets us know that He is there. What a wonderful comfort He is able to give us when we are unsure. Hearing Jesus speak directly to my heart has been the primary burning passion in my life. However, I have discovered that it requires gut-level transparency and honesty with myself and with God.

Revelation knowledge comes from the resurrected Jesus through the Holy Spirit speaking according to the Scripture. He lets you know that He is tracking with you and that He knows you. His *rhema* will nullify the words of fear, condemnation, and lack of hope in your life.

Jesus told Peter about this as recorded in the following Scripture.

Matthew 16:17 says,

> *17 "Jesus answered and said to him, 'Blessed are you, Simon Bar-Jonah, for flesh and blood has not revealed this to you, but My Father who is in heaven.'"*

The two disciples on the Road to Emmaus received revelation knowledge from the resurrected Christ. However, notice, that first Jesus had to extract from them their inner feelings, their unbelief. He asked them, "What things?" When He did that, He caused them to do like we all must do before receiving revelation knowledge, we must pour out our real feelings to the Lord, then He can work. They expressed their grief and disbelief. Jesus asked them in Luke 24:19, "What things (are you sad about)?" Jesus knew why they were sad, but He needed them to express their feelings.

After that, Jesus preached the Scriptures to them, showing them how He was offered as the Lamb of God for the blood covenant, and how He was now alive and speaking life to them.

Luke 24:32 says,

> *32 "And they said to one another, 'Did not our heart burn within us while He talked with us on the road, and while He opened the Scriptures to us?'"*

Hearing God is not reserved for the theologically educated, although there is nothing wrong with that. It is not only for the saint who has "been onin the way" for 30 years, although that helps. It is for the meek, humble, pure in heart, and obedient, perhaps even the broken ones. I heard God speak the first day I got saved, in 1979, and I have been hearing Him ever since. He even speaks to me when pride is in the way so that I may continue to hear Him!

We can neglect the covenant.

Hebrews 2:3 says,

3 "How shall we escape if we neglect so great a salvation, which at the first began to be spoken by the Lord, and was confirmed to us by those who heard Him*."*

We have an inheritance through the blood covenant that is so great that sometimes it is difficult to believe. We have grace by inheritance, but we must position ourselves and respond in a covenant manner to receive the inheritance. Satan is trying to block it, but Jesus is our Judge Advocate, the Mediator.

We have expressed seven primary relationship disciplines in our previous chapters. In this chapter we emphasize the issue of honesty, gut- level honesty. If one were to examine gut- level honesty, it would also translate into humility. This kind of humility and honesty will allow you to hear God speak at a greater level.

Both Cain and Abel heard God speak. Both had instructions from their parents about the blood verses vegetable offerings. What was the difference? Why did Cain hear God, but did not "hear" Him? Cain did not obey, yet even in his disobedience God gave him another chance.

Mark 4:9-12 (Amplified Bible) says,

9 "And He said, He who has ears to hear, let him be hearing [and let him [a] consider, and comprehend].

10 And as soon as He was alone, those who were around Him, with the Twelve [apostles], began to ask Him about the parables.

11 And He said to them, To you has been entrusted the mystery of the kingdom of God [that is, [b] the secret counsels of God which are hidden from the ungodly]; but for those outside [[c] of our circle] everything becomes a parable,

12 In order that they may [indeed] look and look but not see and perceive, and may hear and hear but not grasp and comprehend, lest haply they should turn again, and it ***[their willful rejection of the truth]*** *should be forgiven them."*

I submit that the difference in the "hearing" between Cain and Abel was pride and humility and embracing the truth and not embracing the truth. Notice that Jesus said that when one willfully rejects the truth, that one will not be able to really hear God's voice.

James 4:6 says,

6 "But He gives more grace. Therefore He says:
'God resists the proud, but gives grace to the humble.*'"*

Jesus' blood will continually speak to you if you cooperate. Take time to hear God. Then obey Him as Abel did, even if it means becoming a martyr. Is that not better than becoming a murderer?

Chapter 6
Abraham's Bloody Trench!

In Genesis chapter 14 various kings attacked the city of Sodom, stealing their goods, and kidnapping Lot who was living in Sodom. Abram rescued his cousin Lot and at the same time rescued Sodom's goods. Most likely Abram was greatly out numbered by the enemy. Then after the battle Abram met Melchizedek and the King of Sodom in the Valley of Shaveh – Kings Valley. In opinion, Melchizedek was a manifestation of God, perhaps Jesus Himself.

Genesis 14:17-23 says,

"17 And the king of Sodom went out to meet him at the Valley of Shaveh (that is, the King's Valley), after his return from the defeat of Chedorlaomer and the kings who were with him.

18 Then Melchizedek king of Salem brought out bread and wine; he was the priest of God Most High.

19 And he blessed him and said: "Blessed be Abram of God Most High, Possessor of heaven and earth;

20 And blessed be God Most High, Who has delivered your enemies into your hand." And he gave him a tithe of all.

21 Now the king of Sodom said to Abram, "Give me the persons, and take the goods for yourself."

22 But Abram said to the king of Sodom, "I have raised my hand to the LORD, God Most High, the Possessor of heaven and earth,

23 "that I will take nothing, from a thread to a sandal strap, and that I will not take anything that is yours, lest you should say, 'I have made Abram rich' --"

I believe that the tithe that Abram paid to Melchizedek was more significant than many of us, including myself, can imagine. He gave Melchizedek a tithe on the spoils he obtained in the war on behalf of Sodom. However, later Abram actually gave the spoils back to the King of Sodom.

I believe that Abram knew that Melchizedek was a revelation of Jesus. Remember Jesus said, "Abraham saw my Day and was glad."

John 8:56 says,

"56 "Your father Abraham rejoiced to see My day, and he saw it and was glad.""

Hebrews 7:3 says,

"3 [Melchizedek] without father, without mother, without genealogy, having neither beginning of days nor end of life, but made like the Son of God, remains a priest continually."

From the standpoint of the giver, the tithe cleanses the rest of what he/she owns and receives from the corruption of the world.

I can only guess what prompted Abram to pay tithes. Perhaps Melchizedek instructed him. I have heard that it was a custom in his idol worship. One of my opinions is that is was certainly an act of worship from Abram to God. See Hebrews Chapter 7 for more detail.

However, I can surmise this much that Abram was so completely taken aback with the radical implications of this blood covenant with deity that he would have given or done anything. As it ends up, he did just that in Genesis chapter 22.

Can God's promise be true?
Genesis 15:1, Amplified Bible says,

"After these things, the word of the Lord came to Abram in a vision, saying, Fear not, Abram, I am your Shield, your abundant compensation, and your reward shall be exceedingly great"[4]

---

[4] The reference in this Scriptures is to the Lord as Abram's King.

One may wonder why God may have begun this conversation with "Do not be afraid."

Here is my take on the emotions of both God and Abram. Abram had received a seemingly impossible promise from God in Genesis Chapter 12.

Genesis 12:1-3 says,

"1 Now the LORD had said to Abram: "Get out of your country, From your family And from your father's house, To a land that I will show you.

2 I will make you a great nation; I will bless you And make your name great; And you shall be a blessing.

3 I will bless those who bless you, And I will curse him who curses you; And in you all the families of the earth shall be blessed.""

If I had been in Abram's shoes I would have thought:

"Man, I really went through some terrible warfare and wondered if I or God could ever rescue my relative who had been taken captive by the enemy. Now that it is over, I wonder if that that seemingly impossible promise that God spoke to me back in Chapter 12 about being a great nation could ever come true. This warfare stuff and waiting on promises is really tough!!"

After the war The King of Sodom offered Abram a tremendous financial reward, while Melchizedek offered him a piece of bread and a cup of wine, representing a blood covenant.

Abram knew that his military victory to set Lot free was not in his own power, but by the power of God. When we forsake and cease to depend upon our worldly strengths, (the strength of our flesh, our old unregenerated nature, our inherent dishonesty, human manipulation) and rely entirely on God, through His Word which represents the blood covenant, then God says to us like He said the Abram, "Fear not, I am your Shield, your abundant compensation, and your reward shall be exceedingly great." In other words, "You have depended upon the exchange in the blood and not on the King of Sodom, therefore, I am free to really bless you. I AM your King!"

We can tend to fear how God could possibly keep His very

radical promises to us.

God says "fear not" many times in Scripture. He knows that we have these opportunities to doubt. The only way we can really continue in faith is continue in the Word so that we can continue to hear God speak. Remember the Word is the transfer agent for the blood covenant. Satanic forces will use all their means to make us give up and not stand on the promises God gives us. Abram refused the earthly king's reward, but was promised a reward from the King of Kings.

The bloody trench confirmed the promise.

Abram had some questions about God's promise to bless him and reminded God about his most serious infirmity, being without child.

Genesis 15:2-6 says,

2 "But Abram said, 'Lord GOD, what will You give me, seeing I go childless, and the heir of my house is Eliezer of Damascus?'

3 Then Abram said, 'Look, You have given me no offspring; indeed one born in my house is my heir!'

4 And behold, the word of the LORD came to him, saying, 'This one shall not be your heir, but one who will come from your own body shall be your heir.'

5 Then He brought him outside and said, 'Look now toward heaven, and count the stars if you are able to number them.' And He said to him, 'So shall your descendants be.'

6 And he believed in the LORD, and He accounted it to him for righteousness."

The apostle Paul used Abraham's faith as his main doctrinal reference for our righteousness, and especially in Romans chapter 4.

Romans 4:16 says,

16 "Therefore it is *of faith that* it might *be according to grace, so that the promise might be sure to all the seed, not only to those who are of the law, but also to those who are of the faith of Abraham, who is the father of us all."*

Believing in the finished work of the Cross is what made us righteous, keeps us righteous and what, by grace, transforms our lives to the righteous holiness of God. In Galatians chapter 3, Paul warned his people to not count on their works for continuing their righteousness and to move on with their maturity in Jesus.

Abram was not afraid to ask questions.

Genesis 15:7-11 says,

7 "Then He said to him, 'I am the LORD, who brought you out of Ur of the Chaldeans, to give you this land to inherit it.'

8 And he said, 'Lord GOD, how shall I know that I will inherit it?'

9 So He said to him, 'Bring Me a three-year-old heifer, a three-year-old female goat, a three-year-old ram, a turtledove, and a young pigeon.'

10 Then he brought all these to Him and cut them in two, down the middle, and placed each piece opposite the other; but he did not cut the birds in two.

11 And when the vultures came down on the carcasses, Abram drove them away."

The blood covenant ditch was prepared.

The animal carcasses were cut in halves and set on each side of the ditch to bleed into it. Blood would flow into the ditch and both covenant parties would wade through the blood.

The Lord did not directly answer his question, but went directly to demonstrate His answer through the blood covenant. It should be the same with us. Often we want God to do this thing or that thing, and we need to go back to see what He has already done through the blood covenant. To see what is already ours, we need to pray Ephesians 1:16-20, that the eyes of our hearts may see revelation knowledge, the very personal rhema of God speaking to us. The three parts of this Ephesians Scripture that God suggests that He wants us to see are:

1. His purpose for our calling and for our lives.

2. His inheritance to equip us for living out that calling.

3. His power to bring about both of the above; the power of the resurrection!

I believe that God wanted Abram to see the finished work of the Cross, just as He wants us to see and believe.
When we see the finished work, then we can concentrate on our calling. We are called to abide in the Vine as in John chapter 15, or in other words, to be in strong real-time communion and fellowship with Jesus. John 15 goes on to say that when we keep that relationship right, then fruit happens in our lives. First, fruit for our character. Then, fruit for our provisions, and finally fruit to extend the Kingdom. We are not to be task oriented, but rather we need to be relationship oriented. We turn things upside down so many times and concentrate on doing this or that for God, and often we forsake the relationships that are so important in our lives, including the main one, with God Himself.

When your relationships are right, God's fruit will animate your tasks! I cannot help but to comment here: the primary issue for relationships with others and with God is truth! Too many people try to maintain relationships without honesty; it will not work! Also, God will not tolerate it! His name is Truth! You will be unable to really *see* God and receive His revelation knowledge without *absolute truth!*

God speaks in the dark, in the ditch.

Genesis 15:12-17 says,

12 "Now when the sun was going down, a deep sleep fell upon Abram; and behold, horror and great darkness fell upon him.

13 Then He said to Abram: 'Know certainly that your descendants will be strangers in a land that is not theirs, and will serve them, and they will afflict them four hundred years.

14 And also the nation whom they serve I will judge; afterward they shall come out with great possessions.

15 Now as for you, you shall go to your fathers in peace; you shall be buried at a good old age.

16 But in the fourth generation they shall return here, for the iniquity of the Amorites is not yet complete.'

17 And it came to pass, when the sun went down and it was dark, that behold, there appeared a smoking oven and a burning torch that passed between those pieces."

The following is what most likely happened in those days in the blood covenant ditch.

Each party would walk the ditch towards the other, each proclaiming the blessings if the covenant conditions were kept and the curses if the conditions were not kept. As they reached each other they would often even press an open wound to the other's open wound, often in their wrists. They would exchange coats, weapons and pledges. Sometimes they would exchange rings and signets. They would exchange weaknesses and strengths and they would become more closely related than their "milk" brothers.

Why did God put Abram to sleep?

If Abram had walked through this blood covenant ditch to exchange his curses for God's blessings, it would not have worked. Why? It was because Abram was unable to keep his end of the bargain. He would have failed in the promise, or at least his children would have failed, and for sure, you and I, as his spiritual children have failed.

How did God deal with this? How did God, in His mercy and passion to bless Abram and you and me, pull this off?

I submit that the two persons who walked the blood covenant ditch were the Holy Spirit, representing the Father, and Jesus, representing Abram and you and me! Notice, the two people were a "smoking oven and a burning torch." Abram saw this entire ceremony while in a deep sleep; he had little to do with it. Perhaps one of the persons in the ditch was Melchizedek, a pre-figure of Jesus Himself.

Upon looking up the Hebrew implications of the words "smoking oven" and "burning torch" they seems to indicate the fire of God's wrath. We know that God's entire wrath was put upon Jesus at the Cross in order to allow God to offer us His blessing. That is what happened in a pre-figure (a shadow of the future work of Jesus) in that bloody trench.

I don't think that it is a stretch to say that God appeared unto Abram as recorded in Genesis chapters 12-15 as the incarnated Jesus, the crucified and resurrected One. Many Scriptures tell us that God never changes.

James 1:17 says,

17 "Every good gift and every perfect gift is from above, and comes down from the Father of lights, with whom there is no variation or shadow of turning."

We also know that Jesus was crucified before the foundation of the world (Revelation 13:8). In John 8:56 Jesus said that Abraham saw His incarnation.

Paraphrasing the unsaid message may be like this: "Okay son, I want to bless you with children so that I may have my purpose done on this earth, which is to purchase mankind back from Satan. It is going to take the life of My Son to accomplish this because He is the only perfect One with whom I can make covenant. If you were to walk this ditch, you would fail, you would be without child and My Messiah could not come to redeem you and your descendants. But if My Son, Jesus, were to walk this ditch on your behalf, then when you and your descendants do indeed fail, My Son will die on their behalf." Now that is Good News!

How could God die on behalf of Abraham's descendants? God would have to become God-incarnate!

John 1:1-4, 14 says,

1 "In the beginning was the Word, and the Word was with God, and the Word was God.

2 He was in the beginning with God.
3 All things were made through Him, and without Him nothing was made that was made.
4 In Him was life, and the life was the light of men."

14 "And the Word became flesh and dwelt among us, and we beheld His glory, the glory as of the only begotten of the Father, full of grace and truth."

Abram's main activities for this blood covenant ceremony were:

1. Obeying God to cut and prepare the animals.
2. To keep the vultures away from the covenant promise (spiritual warfare). After that he fell asleep.
3. To believe the unbelievable, the promise. To believe that God was offering to exchange His very life, the life of His Son, for Abram's life of being childless. Romans chapter 4 states that Abraham believed beyond human hope, believed that God, who calls those things that be not as though they were, could perform that which He promised. Also, in the exchange was the promise that Abram's descendants would receive the Holy Spirit, the very personhood of God in their spirit.

God speaks His covenant purposes and promises.

Genesis 15:18-21 says,

18 "On the same day the LORD made a covenant with Abram, saying: 'To your descendants I have given this land, from the river of Egypt to the great river, the River Euphrates –
19 the Kenites, the Kenezzites, the Kadmonites,
20 the Hittites, the Perizzites, the Rephaim,
21 the Amorites, the Canaanites, the Girgashites, and the Jebusites.'"

What was the significance of this blood covenant ceremony?

What did Abram see? What was the real meaning in walking the blood trench?
The Man (Jesus) in the ditch was Abraham's seed but was also Deity. What must have Abraham thought? In the blood covenant exchange Abram received forgiveness, i.e., the cutting away of his very sin nature, his very character, his very personhood. This extends far beyond merely the removal of sin, as we often characterize it. For instance, we can be very grateful that when we fail in our lives, when we perform in a way that is not like the character of God, that God forgives us, or removes that particular transgression. However, deeper forgiveness is experienced in the fact that not only are our "sins" forgiven, but our "sin nature" is removed, that being our very old carnal flesh nature. It is removed, or "forgiven," going into Jesus and we receive His nature in exchange.

When we receive revelation on this, then we experience our true identity.
When we experience our true identity, then our lives will line up, little by little, with God's holiness. When this occurs, then we can resist the devil and accomplish spiritual warfare for our families, the world and ourselves. We need all three: Sit, Walk, and Stand. Ephesians 2:6, 4:1, and 6:11.

Experiencing our new identity has far reaching effects. Our sin is no longer ours it is His. Our cancer and other infirmities are no longer ours; they are His. Our failures are no longer ours, they are His.

What was the real, the true bottom line, promise to Abram?

Galatians 3:13-14 says that God promised the Holy Spirit to Abraham's descendants. What does this mean? I submit that the Holy Spirit is the very person of God and God promised that He Himself, through the Holy Spirit, would be Abram's inheritance via this blood covenant. The other side of this coin is that God's inheritance would be the very spirit of Abram and Abram's descendants, which is a spirit separated from God. This is what happened to Jesus on the Cross. He was separated from God the

Father and the Holy Spirit so that you and I could inherit the very personhood of God Himself.

Galatians 3:14 (Amplified Bible) says,

14 "To the end that through [their receiving] Christ Jesus, the blessing [promised] to Abraham might come upon the Gentiles, so that we through faith might [all] receive [the realization of] the promise of the [Holy] Spirit."

The true promise to Abram, and to you and me, was the Holy Spirit. To put it in other terms, it was to receive the very nature and character and personhood of God into the human race, at least to Abram's descendants (those who believe and have the faith of Abram).

This is The Great Exchange of Identity!

This is the very bottom line of the blood covenant exchange, His Spirit for our spirit. It was not even a restoration of what Adam had lost, for Adam had forsaken the Spirit of God prior to the resurrection of Jesus. Now we receive the Holy Spirit after the resurrection, and the very personhood of the resurrected Jesus, over Whom death and Satan has no more dominion or power! Praise His name forever!

Our inheritance is not simply the blessings that come from God (healing, removal of shame and guilt, removal of the curses that came with our old nature). Our inheritance is far beyond, no matter how exhaustive one makes the list of blessings. Our inheritance is Christ Himself, through the Holy Spirit.

To Moses He said, "I AM." To Abram He said, "I AM in the ditch with you right now. I am swearing to receive your curse and give you My resurrected blessing." To you and me He is saying the same thing! "I AM in the ditch with you, receiving your infirmity, your curse and giving you My blessing."

God cannot lie, nor does He change.

Hebrews 6:17 says,

17 "Thus God, determining to show more

> *abundantly to the heirs of promise the immutability of His counsel, confirmed* it *by an oath."*

You may ask: "If this is so complete, if this blood covenant is so inclusive, if it was to Abraham's seed, and if his seed is Christ and if I have Christ, then why is this not working for me?"

I am glad you asked. You may be thinking that this whole thing is too good to be true, or perhaps you think that you are not worthy enough to experience this great exchange. Maybe you have heard about this and you think it is for others, or maybe you have heard this and think that it is too radical and that those who expound it are just faith freaks. Maybe you have never heard of it. It is called the Gospel, the Good News!

Listen!

1. The blood covenant on your behalf is complete, there is nothing left out, there is nothing that has yet to be accomplished.
2. Notice, however, that even with the promise to Abram in Genesis chapter 15, that God told him that there would be a time of apparent failure. He told him that the Hebrew nation would go into Egyptian bondage for 400 years and then would come out.
3. God works His works on the basis of death and resurrection. One cannot receive the blessing of resurrection without the pain of death.
4. In the experience of "death" during your walk with Jesus you will also notice that you have an antagonist, an enemy to your inheritance: Satan and his team of fallen angels and demons. Abram was called to chase away the vultures from the blood covenant ceremony, that being a type of our standing against the devils that are attempting to block our inheritance.
5. You must experientially inherit the blood covenant through the Word of God planted in your heart as in Mark chapter 4. John 6:63 confirms this idea. Also notice in Mark chapter 4 in the parable about the Word of God, that Jesus emphasizes that seeds do not grow overnight. He stated in verse 4:23-24 that we have the responsibility of hearing and taking responsibility for what we

hear; i.e., obeying what we hear and keeping it as a seed in our heart. Notice in Mark 4:26-32 that Jesus warns that the seed starts out very small, and then takes time to grow into the fruit intended.

6. Jesus warned in Mark 4:14-20 that Satan would use all his resources to steal the seed of the Word. Going through the process of spiritual warfare and of continual death and resurrection is called "overcoming." This is our calling here on earth.

While on the Isle of Patmos, John spoke one common theme to each post-resurrection church as recorded in the Book of Revelation. He ended each of his letters with an exhortation that they become overcomers. It is God calling to all of us saying, "Will anybody sign up for this Overcoming Ministry I have? It pays well, good fringe benefits, life insurance, a promise for eternity, but in the meantime you may not be too comfortable. You see, I have gained the victory over your enemies, as I promised Abraham, but now you, My Body, must exercise that victory over the circumstances and enemies in your realm of influence. But fear not!"

A major part of our spiritual warfare responsibility lies in the proclamation of God's Word to the spiritual enemy.

The Good News is radical!

It is a complete exchange of your personhood for the Holy Spirit, or His personhood. It is the Great Identity Exchange! However, not all people experience the radical exchange. Some don't believe, some are lazy, and others give up while Satan is stealing the seed of the Word that Jesus plants into their hearts.

Chapter 7
Abram's Response to The Covenant

God did not create us as robots. He respects our personal choice and our independent volition. He never forces Himself on anybody. It has been said that the Holy Spirit is manifested as a dove to show us that He can be easily chased away if we do not welcome Him.

In Genesis chapter 15, Abram was called to play a very small part in the blood covenant. He was put to sleep while the two forms of Deity walked through the blood covenant ditch. However, in chapter 17, Abram is called upon to take a very active part in the covenant. It is interesting that this takes place after Abram's episode in Genesis chapter 16, birthing Ishmael with Sarai's maidservant Hagar. God uses this story to warn us about the dangers of the works of our flesh and thinking that we are helping God with His promises by acting presumptuously. We can so easily create "Ishmaels" thinking that we are helping with God's work. To avoid this, we need to learn about God's fruit program. (See our book Grow or Die [5])

God's covenant takes two parties even though He has done the great work. There is still a work that we must perform and that is exercising our free choice to receive Him, to believe Him, to obey Him and to allow Him to do His sanctifying work in us. These responses that we will be discussing in this chapter brings the power of His cross, His grace and His fruit into our realm of influence. The blessings of the Blood Covenant is realized when we take up our cross.

Mark 8:34 says,

"34 When He had called the people to Himself, with His disciples also, He said to them, "Whoever desires to come after Me, let him deny himself, and take up his cross, and follow Me."

In Genesis chapter 17:1-14, God is refreshing His promises to Abram.

---

[5] http://www.isob-bible.org/component/content/article.html?id=615

Genesis 17:1-8 says,

1 "When Abram was ninety-nine years old, the LORD appeared to Abram and said to him, 'I am Almighty God; walk before Me and be blameless.

2 And I will make My covenant between Me and you, and will multiply you exceedingly.'

3 Then Abram fell on his face, and God talked with him, saying:

4 'As for Me, behold, My covenant is with you, and you shall be a father of many nations.

5 No longer shall your name be called Abram, but your name shall be Abraham; for I have made you a father of many nations.

6 I will make you exceedingly fruitful; and I will make nations of you, and kings shall come from you.

7 And I will establish My covenant between Me and you and your descendants after you in their generations, for an everlasting covenant, to be God to you and your descendants after you.

8 Also I give to you and your descendants after you the land in which you are a stranger, all the land of Canaan, as an everlasting possession; and I will be their God.'"

Now God asks Abraham to keep his end of the covenant.
Genesis 17:9-21 says,

"9 And God said to Abraham: "As for you, you shall keep My covenant, you and your descendants after you throughout their generations.

10 "This is My covenant which you shall keep, between Me and you and your descendants after you: Every male child among you shall be circumcised;

11 "and you shall be circumcised in the flesh of your foreskins, and it shall be a sign of the covenant between Me and you.

12 "He who is eight days old among you shall be circumcised, every male child in your generations, he who is born in your house or bought with money from any foreigner who is not your descendant.

13 "He who is born in your house and he who is bought with your money must be circumcised, and My covenant shall be in your flesh for an everlasting covenant.

14 "And the uncircumcised male child, who is not circumcised in the flesh of his foreskin, that person shall be cut off from his people; he has broken My covenant."

15 Then God said to Abraham, "As for Sarai your wife, you shall not call her name Sarai, but Sarah shall be her name.

16 "And I will bless her and also give you a son by her; then I will bless her, and she shall be a mother of nations; kings of peoples shall be from her."

17 Then Abraham fell on his face and laughed, and said in his heart, "Shall a child be born to a man who is one hundred years old? And shall Sarah, who is ninety years old, bear a child?"

18 And Abraham said to God, "Oh, that Ishmael might live before You!"

19 Then God said: "No, Sarah your wife shall bear you a son, and you shall call his name Isaac; I will establish My covenant with him for an everlasting covenant, and with his descendants after him.

20 "And as for Ishmael, I have heard you. Behold, I have blessed him, and will make him fruitful, and will multiply him exceedingly. He shall beget twelve princes, and I will make him a great nation.

21 "But My covenant I will establish with Isaac, whom Sarah shall bear to you at this set time next year.""

How does this apply to our lives? This must have been another great challenge to Abraham's faith!

Abraham was blessed in order to be a blessing. God did not bless him, nor does He bless us with the New Birth in order to have us return to our old nature, our old lifestyle, our old idols, and our self-seeking and selfish ways. He blessed us to be a blessing to others. He gave us His character, His Spirit, so that we could do His work on this earth. Two of the main purposes of the blood covenant with God, besides our eternal well being, is to have us cooperate in bringing His Kingdom to this earth, and to enjoy an intimate relationship with God. However, He does not demand that from us. Even though He craves that intimacy with us, He gives us a free choice.

I cannot explain why some people seem to stop short with God and not allow Him to work everything He wants to do with and in us. I do know that we always have choices and that my personal choices have always been out of love for Him. Sure I am thankful daily for what He *did* for me, but I am more motivated by Who He *is*! Romans chapter 2 states that the love of God leads us to repentance. God prefers to draw us with His love rather than guilt and condemnation. Yet some people do not respond.

One great example is in the Book of Hosea.

God tarried with Israel, who was depicted as a prostitute in that setting. Yet He woos her with His love. At the end of Hosea God uses the following prophecy for Israel and for you and me.

Hosea 14:4-8 says,

4 "I will heal their backsliding, I will love them freely, for My anger has turned away from him.

5 I will be like the dew to Israel; He shall grow like the lily, and lengthen his roots like Lebanon.

6 His branches shall spread; His beauty shall be like an olive tree, and his fragrance like Lebanon.

7 Those who dwell under his shadow shall return; they shall be revived like grain, and grow like a vine. Their scent shall be like the wine of Lebanon.

8 Ephraim shall say, 'What have I to do anymore with idols?' I have heard and observed him. I am like a green cypress tree; Your fruit is found in Me."

God was saying, "Once they see Me, they will turn from their idols." The Old Testament points to the true circumcision, which **is** heart circumcision. The New Testament confirms it. This is how this subject applies to us.

Deuteronomy 30:6 says,

6 "And the LORD your God will circumcise your heart and the heart of your descendants, to love the LORD your God with all your heart and with all your soul, that you may live."

Notice that the purpose of this heart circumcision is so that you and your descendants may love the LORD with all your heart and soul, and that you may "live." Notice also that spiritual circumcision is in the foreskin of your heart, the spiritual procreation force. Notice that it goes to your descendants as well as it did to Abraham's. But we must respond in faith, the kind of faith that Abraham had. That was faith that was beyond his wildest imagination!

What Abram did in the circumcision in his flesh is a type and shadow or our spiritual circumcision.

Genesis 17:24-27 says,

24 "Abraham was *ninety-nine years old when he was circumcised in the flesh of his foreskin.*

25 And Ishmael his son was *thirteen years old when he was circumcised in the flesh of his foreskin.*

26 That very same day Abraham was circumcised, and his son Ishmael;

27 and all the men of his house, born in the house or bought with money from a foreigner, were circumcised with him."

The New Testament explains spiritual circumcision.
Romans 2:29 says,

29 "But he is *a Jew who* is *one inwardly; and circumcision* is that *of the heart, in the Spirit, not in the letter; whose praise* is *not from men but from God."*

Spiritual circumcision is simply the removal of our old nature replaced with the Holy Spirit. The Word speaks to us in Colossians that our spiritual circumcision is also a tremendous gift from God. Not only is it a gift, it says that it is past tense, something that happened at our New Birth. While this is true, like Abram, we must confirm this great blood covenant by confirming our spiritual circumcision. We must know for sure that this is a finished work. God has circumcised our spirit, our heart, through the New Birth; however, our mind, the old nature, fights against this. We need to take our thoughts captive and bring them to the cross. We discuss this in more detail on the following pages. God told Abram that if he did not keep this rite, that the covenant would be broken. That, on the surface, sounds like a paradox when compared to the bloody ditch in Genesis chapter 15 where God did all the work.

There is a tender balance between just recognizing the free gift and truly walking in it, receiving it, believing it, acting on it and giving ourselves to it. If we don't do our part, we are forsaking the benefits and purpose of the covenant. Many people find themselves in bondage feeling forsaken by God. If we only knew how God, in His great love, is longing for us to receive, we would not doubt Him.

Caution.

Human beings were created by God to bear some type of spiritual agriculture. We have no choice, be **will** bear either good fruit or some sore of weeds, or as the Bible calls it, tares. Notice that Abram, while still uncircumcised bore the child Ishmael, which turned out to be not profitable. It was only after Abram's circumcision that he bore Isaac, which was God's intended fruit.

Therefore it is the same with our spiritual circumcision.

If we are living according to our old flesh nature we will bear tares, or unprofitable crops which will be burned. But if we are living according to the Spirit, we will be fruit bearers. Mark chapter 4 and Matthew chapter 13 both are about the Parable of the Sower. Mark 4:11 states that this Parable is the "mystery of the Kingdom of God. Matthew goes into more detail regarding fruit and tares. Jesus comments that the tares in this parable as "sons of the wicked one." However our tares can also be circumstances in our lives that come about because we are not in the fruit bearing, circumcised mode.

Matthew 13:18-30 says,

"18 "Therefore hear the parable of the sower:

19 "When anyone hears the word of the kingdom, and does not understand it, then the wicked one comes and snatches away what was sown in his heart. This is he who received seed by the wayside.

20 "But he who received the seed on stony places, this is he who hears the word and immediately receives it with joy;

21 "yet he has no root in himself, but endures only for a while. For when tribulation or persecution arises because of the word, immediately he stumbles.

22 "Now he who received seed among the thorns is he who hears the word, and the cares of this world and the deceitfulness of riches choke the word, and he becomes unfruitful.

23 "But he who received seed on the good ground is he who hears the word and understands it, who indeed bears fruit and produces: some a hundredfold, some sixty, some thirty."

24 Another parable He put forth to them, saying: "The kingdom of heaven is like a man who sowed good seed in his field;

25 "but while men slept, his enemy came and sowed tares among the wheat and went his way.

26 "But when the grain had sprouted and produced a crop, then the tares also appeared.

27 "So the servants of the owner came and said to him, 'Sir, did you not sow good seed in your field? How then does it have tares?'

28 "He said to them, 'An enemy has done this.' The servants said to him, 'Do you want us then to go and gather them up?'

29 "But he said, 'No, lest while you gather up the tares you also uproot the wheat with them.

30 'Let both grow together until the harvest, and at the time of harvest I will say to the reapers, "First gather together the tares and bind them in bundles to burn them, but gather the wheat into my barn."'""

Our spiritual circumcision is a past tense finished work. However we must do our part to believe and apply that truth to our lives.

Colossians 2:11-15 says,

11 "In Him you were [past tense] also circumcised with the circumcision made without hands, by putting off the body of the sins of the flesh, by the circumcision of Christ,

12 buried with Him in baptism, in which you also were raised with Him through faith in the working of God, who raised Him from the dead.

13 And you, being dead in your trespasses and the uncircumcision of your flesh, He has made alive together with Him, having forgiven you all trespasses,

14 having wiped out the handwriting of requirements that was against us, which was contrary to us. And He has taken it out of the way, having nailed it to the cross.

15 Having disarmed principalities and powers, He made a public spectacle of them, triumphing over them in it."

I submit that taking up our cross daily confirms and establishes our spiritual circumcision. Even though it may be a past tense fact, we do not realize the benefits until we make the choice to deny our old nature.

I believe that there is a spiritual law that goes like this: "The more you take up your cross, the more benefits of His cross you will receive." I believe that we can remain spiritually bankrupt just because we do not take up our cross. I am not sure what this will feel like when we get to Heaven, but I can tell you that I do not want to be guilty of rejecting the great blessings and gifts of God that He so painfully paid for. Do you?

This "taking up our cross" can take various forms for different people. It can also be a greatly misunderstood "religious" term that can be abused. However, I believe that we can generalize it as follows:

1. We respond to God's great love and we have a great desire to love God back. Therefore, we continue in His Word to communicate with Him. While in His Word we see the pattern of holiness, the character of Jesus.

2. We humble ourselves to use the Word as a mirror to detect those areas of our lives that do not resemble God's character. The Holy Spirit will actively work in us to bring those issues to the surface.

3. We are simply honest. We agree with God about our condition and confess it to Him. The word "confess" carries with it the meaning "to agree with." I have personally seen horrible spiritual disasters in people who did not exercise gut level honesty!

4. As we confess our sin, the circumcision is made complete experientially, or at least it is carried to the next step.

1 John 1:9 says,

9 "If we confess our sins, He is faithful and just to forgive us our sins and to cleanse us from all unrighteousness."

The terms *cleansing from all unrighteousness* and *forgiveness* carries with them the root meaning of cutting way with a surgeon's knife. That is circumcision. Yes, we are already spiritually circumcised, but with each process we are experientially circumcised.

Henry Clay Trumbull, for most of his life, researched blood covenants in ancient cultures, including Bible cultures. In his book, <u>The Blood Covenant</u>[6] he states:

> *The recognition of the covenant of blood in the rite of circumcision, throws light on an obscure passage in the life of Moses, as recorded in Exodus 4:20-26. Moses, himself a child of the covenant, had neglected the circumcision of his own first-born; and so he had been unfaithful to the covenant of Abraham. While on his way from the Wilderness of Sinai to Egypt with a message from God to Pharaoh, concerning the un-covenanted first-born of the Egyptians, Moses was met by a startling providence and came face to face with death – possible with a bloody death of some sort. "The Lord met him, and sought to kill him," (Exodus 4:24) it is said. It seems to have been perceived, both by Moses and his wife, that they were being cut off from a farther share in God's covenant plan for the descendants of Abraham, because of their failure to conform to their obligations in the covenant of Abraham.*
>
> *"Then Zipporah took a sharp stone and cut off the foreskin of her son and cast it at Moses' feet, and said, 'Surely you are a husband of blood to me!' So He let him go. Then she said, 'You are a husband of blood!' -- because of the circumcision" (Exodus 4:25-26).*
>
> *So He, the Lord, let Moses alone, He spared him, as one newly true to the covenant of Abraham, and newly*

---

[6] H. Clay Trumbull. *The Blood Covenant*. Impact Books Inc. Kirkwood, MO., 1975, pages 221-223.

safe within its bounds. Then Zipporah said again, "A bridegroom of blood (husband of blood) are thou, because of the circumcision."

The Hebrew word "khathan," here translated "bridegroom or husband of blood," has as its root idea, the binding through severing, the covenanting by blood; an idea that is in the marriage-rite, as the Orientals view it, and that is in the rite of circumcision, also. Indeed, in the Arabic, the corresponding term (khatan) is applied interchangeably to one who is a relation by the way of one's wife, and to one who is circumcised. Hence, the words of Zipporah would imply that, by this rite of circumcision, she and her child were brought into blood-covenant relations with the descendants of Abraham, and her husband also was now saved to that covenant; whereas before they were in danger of being covenanted to a bloody death.

It is as though Zipporah had said: "We are now newly covenanted to each other, and to God, by blood; whereas, but for this, we should have been covenanted to slaughter, or death by blood.

The bottom line.

God was in the bloody trench; He bore the Cross for us. He did the work that only He could do. That was a free gift. He told Abram in Genesis chapter 17 that he needed to do what he could do. For us that means:

1. Knowing that we have been "circumcised" spiritually with the New Birth.

2. Confirming that circumcision by confessing our sin and refusing to let remnants of our old nature to control us. That is also a free gift. It is a miracle, but we need to cooperate, otherwise we could experience the "bloody death" that was on its way to Moses.

Be intense with God. Be real with God. Keep your "knife" handy! The rewards are beyond comprehension. We also have an opportunity to give God a "good day" and bless Him! Looking at

Moses and Zipporah, we can learn that we are in grave danger if we ignore this rite.

Chapter 8
The Blood Covenant Breaks Curses

Genesis 22:1-2 says,

> *1 "Now it came to pass after these things that God tested [to assay]* [7] *Abraham, and said to him, 'Abraham!' And he said, 'Here I am.' Then He said, 'Take now your son, your only son Isaac, whom you love, and go to the land of Moriah, and offer him there as a burnt offering on one of the mountains of which I shall tell you.'"*

There have been many speculations, wonderful sermons and even books on Genesis chapter 22, as to why God asked Abraham to obey such a command to take the life of his promised son Isaac, or the life of any human being.

I submit that Abraham and Sarah were under the curse of being without child. That was one of the most serious and shameful maladies of that age. God gave Abram the promise of having a child, and through that child many nations would be blessed. Abram did his best to obey and follow the Lord, until Genesis chapter 16 when he took matters into his own hands and produced Ishmael. Then in Genesis chapter 21 the supernatural promise was fulfilled; Isaac, the son of promise, was born of barren Sarah and Abraham. One would have thought that the issue of being childless was over. Right? Wrong!

I submit that Isaac and Abraham were still subject to the curse and that they needed to complete the overcoming process with God to destroy the curse. I also need to point out that the curse was not broken until Abraham obeyed God and walked all the way up the hill, raised his knife, and fully expected to slay his son.

That is the way with us. We have to go all the way up our hills because that is where the Lamb was for Abraham and for us. I have personally experienced God dealing this way with my family and some curses we needed to overcome. God spoke this "up the hill" idea to me very clearly.

---

[7] Assay: an examination and analysis of something, chemical testing carried out to determine the composition or a substance of the concentration of various components in a substance, a sample of material for analysis.

Deuteronomy chapter 28 is a good place to study curses and blessings.

A curse is the opposite of a blessing. A blessing is some type of prosperity from God that is the result of good and positive words or deeds. A curse is some type of failure caused or propagated by wicked or negative words or deeds that can be perpetrated by people and satanic beings.

Exodus 34:5-8 says that curses are passed down to future generations

Exodus 34:7 says,

7 "Keeping mercy for thousands, forgiving iniquity and transgression and sin, by no means clearing the guilty, *visiting the iniquity of the fathers upon the children and the children's children to the third and the fourth generation."*

Wouldn't it be nice if we could just read the Bible, discover that we are forgiven and that Jesus took our curse, then say a nice tidy prayer and see the blessings come? Sorry, often it does not work that way, although sometimes it has and can. Curses can be broken by prayer and deliverance instantly, however my experience has been going through the hard times of the overcoming process, much in the same way Abraham did with Isaac.

Now let's refer back to Abraham and Isaac.

Genesis 22:7-17 says,

"7 But Isaac spoke to Abraham his father and said, "My father!" And he said, "Here I am, my son." Then he said, "Look, the fire and the wood, but where is the lamb for a burnt offering?"

8 And Abraham said, "My son, God will provide for Himself the lamb for a burnt offering." So the two of them went together.

9 Then they came to the place of which God had told him. And Abraham built an altar there and placed the wood in order; and he bound Isaac his son and laid him on the altar, upon the wood."

10 And Abraham stretched out his hand and took the knife to slay his son.

11 But the Angel of the LORD called to him from heaven and said, 'Abraham, Abraham!' So he said, 'Here I am.'

12 And He said, 'Do not lay your hand on the lad, or do anything to him; for now I know that you fear God, since you have not withheld your son, your only son, from Me.'

13 Then Abraham lifted his eyes and looked, and there behind him was a ram caught in a thicket by its horns. So Abraham went and took the ram, and offered it up for a burnt offering instead of his son.

14 And Abraham called the name of the place, The-LORD-Will-Provide; as it is said to this day, 'In the Mount of the LORD it shall be provided.'"

15 "Then the Angel of the LORD called to Abraham a second time out of heaven,

16 and said: 'By Myself I have sworn, says the LORD, because you have done this thing, and have not withheld your son, your only son –

17 blessing I will bless you, and multiplying I will multiply your descendants as the stars of the heaven and as the sand which is on the seashore; and your descendants shall possess the gate of their enemies.'"

God's covenant with Abraham promised him a son. Genesis 15:3-17

"3 Then Abram said, "Look, You have given me no offspring; indeed one born in my house is my heir!"

4 And behold, the word of the LORD came to him, saying, "This one shall not be your heir, but one who will come from your own body shall be your heir."

5 Then He brought him outside and said, "Look now toward heaven, and count the stars if you are able to number them." And He said to him, "So shall your descendants be."

6 And he believed in the LORD, and He accounted it to him for righteousness.

7 Then He said to him, "I am the LORD, who brought you out of Ur of the Chaldeans, to give you this land to inherit it."

8 And he said, "Lord GOD, how shall I know that I will inherit it?"

9 So He said to him, "Bring Me a three-year-old heifer, a three-year-old female goat, a three-year-old ram, a turtledove, and a young pigeon."

10 Then he brought all these to Him and cut them in two, down the middle, and placed each piece opposite the other; but he did not cut the birds in two.

11 And when the vultures came down on the carcasses, Abram drove them away.

12 Now when the sun was going down, a deep sleep fell upon Abram; and behold, horror and great darkness fell upon him.

13 Then He said to Abram: "Know certainly that your descendants will be strangers in a land that is not theirs, and will serve them, and they will afflict them four hundred years.

14 "And also the nation whom they serve I will judge; afterward they shall come out with great possessions.

15 "Now as for you, you shall go to your fathers in peace; you shall be buried at a good old age.

16 "But in the fourth generation they shall return here, for the iniquity of the Amorites is not yet complete."

17 And it came to pass, when the sun went down and it was dark, that behold, there appeared a smoking oven and a burning torch that passed between those pieces."

18 On the same day the LORD made a covenant with Abram, saying: "To your descendants I have given this land, from the river of Egypt to the great river, the River Euphrates--"

How did Abraham have so much faith to raise the knife over Isaac?

God had given Abraham a blood covenant in Genesis 15. Given the blood covenant, it did not matter how impossible circumstances looked, Abraham believed in a resurrection.

Hebrews 11:17-19,

"17 By faith Abraham, when he was tested, offered up Isaac, and he who had received the promises offered up his only begotten son,

18 of whom it was said, "In Isaac your seed shall be called,"

19 concluding that God *was* able to raise *him* up, even from the dead, from which he also received him in a figurative sense."

How does this apply to us?

We are in a blood covenant with God through Jesus. It does not matter how impossible circumstances may look. Our curses are often overcome through the same process that God used with Abraham. First the covenant was given, then the promise for deliverance, and then the death and resurrection process.

We have to "put our knife" into our promises, hopes and dreams that the enemy is trying to destroy by curses, and then watch God raise them from the dead. I have done this so many times. It was painful but God came through!

I believe that Genesis chapter 22 and the entire Book of Revelation indicates to us that we realize blessings by overcoming through the death and resurrection process.

Revelation 12:11 says,

> *11 "And they overcame him by the blood of the Lamb and by the word of their testimony, and they did not love their lives to the death."*

A major theme in Revelation is the Scroll.

John wrote Revelation while he was suffering on the Isle of Patmos. He was trying to make some sense out of his life and he owed some explanation to his churches on why they were being persecuted so violently and why some of them were being beheaded and tortured. This is worked out in Oriental Eastern mystic writings in the rest of Revelation as Jesus revealed to John, in picture form something that would show him, and you and me the prophetic victory for his sufferings. I am in no way predicting the historic events for end times by using this mystic message that God included in the Book of Revelation.

In Zechariah 5:1-5 the Scroll is the curse.

Zechariah 5:1-4 says,

"1 Then I turned and raised my eyes, and saw there a flying scroll.

2 And he said to me, "What do you see?" So I answered, "I see a flying scroll. Its length is twenty cubits and its width ten cubits."

3 Then he said to me, "This is the curse that goes out over the face of the whole earth: 'Every thief shall be expelled,' according to this side of the scroll; and, 'Every perjurer shall be expelled,' according to that side of it."

4 "I will send out the curse," says the LORD of hosts; "It shall enter the house of the thief And the house of the one who swears falsely by My name. It shall remain in the midst of his house And consume it, with its timber and stones.""

The Scroll in Revelation 5 at the Throne in Heaven.

Notice in Revelation Chapter 5, there is a word picture of The Father God at the Throne holding the Scroll. We know from the Book of Zechariah the Scroll represents God's inheritance for man and the curse for Satan.

Revelation 5:1-9 says,

"1 And I saw in the right hand of Him who sat on the throne a scroll written inside and on the back, sealed with seven seals.

2 Then I saw a strong angel proclaiming with a loud voice, "Who is worthy to open the scroll and to loose its seals?"

3 And no one in heaven or on the earth or under the earth was able to open the scroll, or to look at it.

4 So I wept much, because no one was found worthy to open and read the scroll, or to look at it.

5 But one of the elders said to me, "Do not weep. Behold, the Lion of the tribe of Judah, the Root of David, has prevailed to open the scroll and to loose its seven seals."

6 And I looked, and behold, in the midst of the throne and of the four living creatures, and in the midst of the elders, stood a Lamb as though it had been slain, having seven horns and seven eyes, which are the seven Spirits of God sent out into all the earth.

7 Then He came and took the scroll out of the right hand of Him who sat on the throne.

8 Now when He had taken the scroll, the four living creatures and the twenty-four elders fell down before the Lamb, each having a harp, and golden bowls full of incense, which are the prayers of the saints.

9 And they sang a new song, saying: "You are worthy to take the scroll, And to open its seals; For You were slain, And have redeemed us to God by Your blood Out of every tribe and tongue and people and nation,"

Hal Lindsey describes the procedure regarding scrolls in ancient times.

Sealing a scroll was a common and important practice in Biblical times. The wills of both Emperor Vespasian and Caesar Augustus were secured with seven seals.

"For such a document, a scribe would procure a long roll of parchment and begin writing. After a period of writing he would stop, roll the parchment enough to cover his words and seal the scroll at that point with wax. Then he would resume writing, stop again, roll the scroll, and add another seal. By the time he was finished, he would have sealed the scroll seven times. The scrolls would be read a section at a time, after each seal was opened.

"Why was this process used? Evidently it was to prevent unauthorized persons from tampering with the scroll or reading and revealing its contents. Only a "worthy" person -- that is, someone with proper authority -- could have legal access to the scroll's message.

"When a Jewish family was required to forfeit its land and possessions through some distress, the property could not be permanently taken from them. Their losses were listed in a scroll and sealed seven times, then the conditions necessary to purchase

back the land and possessions were written on the outside of the scroll. When a qualified redeemer could be found to meet the requirements of reclamation, the one to whom the property had been forfeited was obligated to return the possessions to the original owner."

God asked John to "eat" the Scroll.
Revelation 10:1-2, 8-11 says,

> *"1 I saw still another mighty angel coming down from heaven, clothed with a cloud. And a rainbow was on his head, his face was like the sun, and his feet like pillars of fire.*
> *2 He had a little book open in his hand. And he set his right foot on the sea and his left foot on the land,*
>
> *8 Then the voice which I heard from heaven spoke to me again and said, "Go, take the little book which is open in the hand of the angel who stands on the sea and on the earth."*
> *9 So I went to the angel and said to him, "Give me the little book." And he said to me, "Take and eat it; and it will make your stomach bitter, but it will be as sweet as honey in your mouth."*
> *10 Then I took the little book out of the angel's hand and ate it, and it was as sweet as honey in my mouth. But when I had eaten it, my stomach became bitter.*
> *11 And he said to me, "You must prophesy again about many peoples, nations, tongues, and kings.""*

Why did God have John "eat the Scroll"?

While the seals in the Scroll are being opened, overcoming the curse, we will hear and feel terrible things, even sufferings so great that many will be tempted to believe that Jesus did not overcome their curse. Many will give up.

John felt this as he ate the Book or the Scroll. The redemption inscribed on the outer part of the Scroll tasted good, but when he digested it he tasted the inner parts of the Scroll where the curses were written. I believe that as John tasted the inner parts of the Scroll that he had a personal witness regarding the pain that Jesus incurred at the Cross.

He felt the pain and eternal judgment of those who do not have Jesus to bear their curses. But he also felt the pain and temporary judgment of believers who have given up their overcoming process. It is clear to me both by Scripture (in addition to the Book of Revelation) and by personal experience, and also the experiences of others, that more often than not our overcoming processes must go through death and resurrection. We can feel like the curses have overcome us by looking at the time line coupled with horrible circumstances, but if we hang on to a godly overcoming process, we will prevail for our lives and for His Kingdom. As with John, our task is to stay in the presence of God and in His Word, so that through the overcoming process we will continue to experience God and therefore keep our perseverance. I have often written that "pieces" of His Kingdom are established on earth through our overcoming process.

Up to this point in Revelation six angels appeared and six of the seven Trumpets were sounded.

Revelation 11:15-19

> *"15 Then the seventh angel sounded [the Trumpet]: And there were loud voices in heaven, saying, "The kingdoms of this world have become the kingdoms of our Lord and of His Christ, and He shall reign forever and ever!"*
>
> *16 And the twenty-four elders who sat before God on their thrones fell on their faces and worshiped God,*
>
> *17 saying: "We give You thanks, O Lord God Almighty, The One who is and who was and who is to come, Because You have taken Your great power and reigned.*
>
> *18 The nations were angry, and Your wrath has come, And the time of the dead, that they should be judged, And that You should reward Your servants the prophets and*

the saints, And those who fear Your name, small and great, And should destroy those who destroy the earth."

19 Then the temple of God was opened in heaven, and the ark of His covenant was seen in His temple. And there were lightnings, noises, thunderings, an earthquake, and great hail."

Hang on until the seventh Trumpet and the seventh angel and you will see your curse resurrected and the Kingdom of God advanced because of your overcoming.

Resurrection while still here on earth!

John 11:20-27,44

Now Martha, as soon as she heard that Jesus was coming, went and met Him, but Mary was sitting in the house. Now Martha said to Jesus, "Lord, if You had been here, my brother would not have died. But even now I know that whatever You ask of God, God will give You."

Jesus said to her, "Your brother will rise again."

Martha said to Him, "I know that he will rise again in the resurrection at the last day."

Jesus said to her, "I am the resurrection and the life. He who believes in Me, though he may die, he shall live. And whoever lives and believes in Me shall never die. Do you believe this?"

She said to Him, "Yes, Lord, I believe that You are the Christ, the Son of God, who is to come into the world."

"44 And he who had died came out bound hand and foot with graveclothes, and his face was wrapped with a cloth. Jesus said to them, "Loose him, and let him go.""

Philippians 3:11,

That if possible I may attain to the [spiritual and moral] resurrection [that lifts me] out from among the dead [even while in the body].

Help Wanted

Construction Workers

Limited number of positions open for the construction of New Jerusalem, a City designed by Jehovah God and being built by Jesus of Nazareth. Exceptional pay. The Master has a habit of paying for a full day in compensation for one hour of work. Fringe benefits include health insurance, retirement with full pay, protection from all forms of evil, relief from need and want; free emotional and psychological counseling.

Job consists of using The Master's own tools and property to add several finishing sections to The City, called New Jerusalem.

Qualifications: Applicants must be willing to submit to being changed (during a probation period) from a foolish to a wise virgin in the context of Matthew chapter 25.

Warning-Disclosure: Many former applicants have been disappointed and quit during the probation period when they discovered that the Master's tools were their problems, perplexities, infirmities and handicaps which have been strained through The Master's Cross, washed and coated in His Blood, disarmed and defused of all evil and their ability to harm, and converted to a highly valuable construction material known as jewels through an amazing, but time proven process known as "overcoming." Many preferred to stay as foolish virgins and see these "tools" as enemies. When their Master returned at the end of the probation period, they did not even recognize Him.

After the conversion process from foolish to wise, the few that made it discovered that they had been carrying around the most valuable raw material in the universe. When they plunged these problems into the Cross the very nature of these former problems had actually been changed from bitter to sweet, from enemy to friend, and their reward was beyond explanation. Some actually reported that they saw wolves fellowshipping with lambs.

Interested parties should contact:

The Holy Spirit

Chapter 9
Have You Been a Slave and Didn't Know It?

Slavery is the very foundation of the world system and Satan's kingdom.

Slavery puts others to hard labor to accomplish something profitable for the slave owner. In the natural sense it brought great profit to the owners of plantations to have had slaves work the crops. They didn't have to pay them normal wages; they simply needed to give them the basic food and shelter to keep them alive so that they could continue to work.

Spiritual slavery puts humans to work for Satan's profit, to accomplish his rebellious purposes. He puts God's greatest creation to work for him and binds man in such a position so that he does not even recognize God much less fellowship with Him. If God is recognized then He is portrayed as a mean hard taskmaster.

When Jacob and his twelve sons first settled in Egypt, there were only seventy Hebrews in total. Hundreds of years later there were two and a half million Hebrews. Joseph enjoyed much favor with the ruler of Egypt, Pharaoh. Hundreds of years later the Egyptians were working the Hebrews as their slaves. (Exodus 1:8-11). You may recall in previous chapters that God told Abraham that his family would go into bondage into a strange land. This did not catch God off guard.

Exodus 1:13-14 says,

> *13 "So the Egyptians made the children of Israel serve with rigor.*
>
> *14 And they made their lives bitter with hard bondage – in mortar, in brick, and in all manner of service in the field. All their service in which they made them serve* was *with rigor."*

Real slavery is spiritual slavery, something that has someone in bondage on the inside. I believe that these Hebrews, like the rest of us, were slaves before they became slaves. I believe that they were already spiritual slaves and did not know it. Perhaps it is

God's mercy that allows people to experience great pain in their lives just so that they will cry out to Him. Then in His mercy He can point out that the true issue is spiritual slavery and He can then go to work to solve the true problem.

What are some of the symptoms of the slavery mindset?
Give yourself a check-up. However, as you go through this, please keep in mind that God does not want you to become condemned or shamed if any of these attributes are found. He is simply trying to get you to see the invisible slavery so that He can set you free. Just imagine yourself in a penitentiary with Jesus at the gate holding the key to your release. Don't be ashamed of the symptoms, perhaps addictions, improper behavior or the other attributes listed here, just get out! Allow Him to set you free!

There is a good chance that you inherited your slavery, and even if you were the cause of it, you must know the love of God. He uses His love to bring you to Him, not condemnation. God does not blame! He took the blame for you! Run to Him with your slavery and allow Him to heal you! He takes you just the way you are, but He loves you too much to leave you that way!

One of the sneakiest types of slavery is slavery to oneself, otherwise known as selfishness. When we continue to yield to our own selfish desires, we become slaves to our old fallen nature, the flesh.

A lack of identity is the primary attribute of a slave.

Slaves obtain their identity from something or someone else besides God. That is why you see people in the American culture running around trying to get fancy cars, having certain types of friends, dressing a certain way, being part of a movie star's fan club, etc. Some obtain their identity by being on a certain corporate payroll, or living in an elite neighborhood. In some cultures it may include belonging to the proper tribe or family. They are trying to define who they are by how they look, what they drive and with whom they associate.

How are we supposed to receive our identity? I believe that God created us to receive our identity through having a relationship with another being. We are designed to become like the person with whom we become intimate. We receive our identity from whom we obtain our needs. God wants us to become intimate with Him in order to receive our identity from Him. He has taken up residence inside of us. If that does not give you identity, self-worth and dignity, then nothing will!

During the first century, the Romans dragged people from their homes and made them slaves. Families were forever separated, never again to see their parents, children, brothers, sisters or spouses. Most likely the women and men were raped and beaten. They completely lost their identity.

Identity though one's performance is typical of slavery.

From the slave's point of view his life was now different. He had no identity of his own; he was a non-person. The only thing that he had left was what he could do in his work. The only scale or measure of who he was now was the way he performed his task. If his master looked at him with pleasure because his task was done well, he could feel some self-esteem. Even if another slave admired his work, or perhaps someone else up the ladder of authority gave him one compliment, one measure of "well done," he could feel good about himself.

His life was now a formula. (How I perform) + (how you feel about my performance) = (my self-worth).

The human being was created by God to obtain his worth from God's unconditional love. Now exactly the opposite has happened; humans feel like all love is totally conditioned upon how they perform, and worse, how their masters feel about their performance.

Is this where critical people come from?

If this slave's performance is not very good, then he feels condemned. On the flip side, if the slave sees another person whose performance is not perfect, he is quick to criticize and condemn. I believe in this way, the slave is devaluing the other person and in some way feels that he is giving value to himself. God set up a very powerful way to remind those who judge others to feel the pain of it. Be careful with your judgments, they come back at you with at least the same intensity you used if not more. Jesus said in Matthew 7:1, "Judge not that you be not judged." Then later in verses 3 and 4 He explained that your judgment is like a beam compared to the other person's faults, their splinters, that you are judging. The person you are judging may be wrong, but your judgment is even worse.

James 4:11 says,

> *11 "Do not speak evil of one another, brethren. He who speaks evil of a brother and judges his brother, speaks evil of the law and judges the law. But if you judge the law, you are not a doer of the law but a judge."*

Slaves are "men-pleasers" (Ephesians 6:5). They are constantly trying to get the applause and approval of other people. Their work has no other meaning. If their boss, their parents or teachers are pleased with their work, they feel good about their self worth; if not, they feel like "nothings." They are always attempting to get friends who will give them their identity and self-worth.

Slaves work for "eye-service" *(Ephesians 6:5).*

While they are being watched, they work hard, but as soon as their authorities turn their backs, they goof off. They hold in their resentment of their authority figures. They criticize them and bring them down all the time.

Slaves Complain. They always blame their problems on other people. In their minds, their horrible state of being is always somebody else's fault. This often manifests itself by devaluing others with gossip and criticism.

Some slaves become very good at manipulation. They learn how to please and even "love" others, so that they will be "loved back."

Slaves do not like obeying authority. They have learned that authority is bad; they hate their authority figures.

Slaves control others. They have no authority, so they are always manipulating others in order to serve their own needs.

Some slaves use their sheer brute force, like shouting and screaming in order to get others to conform.

Slaves have no self-esteem. They use other people, religion, amusement and immorality, which are some of the same things the Hebrews used in the desert to achieve some sense of self worth.

Slaves become addicts. If you are addicted to food, drugs, alcohol, pornography, or even seemingly more benign things like newspapers, TV, computer games, etc., you are a slave. God has the power to make you free. Do not live in condemnation for your failure.

My testimony about alcohol consumption.

Please take what I say here with mercy and grace, as what I say is primarily my personal testimony and is not intended to be absolute doctrine for the Body of Christ.

I have read scientific studies, which show that alcohol consumption, even in the smallest amounts, contributes to and even causes many types of cancer in adults, and deformities in babies while in the womb. Medical people who deal with brain issues have told me that even small intakes of alcohol destroy brain cells. Ask a nurse who cares for dementia patients in a nursing home setting. They have personally shown me patients who have been so affected. Ask a Christian believer in Africa or Haiti who has been delivered from witchcraft. He will tell you how his former slave masters kept him in bondage with alcohol.

Some people have called me "religious" and intolerant for such a belief. I can only say what the Lord has revealed to me and spoken to me for my own life. He spoke to me, I believe, for my own benefit. I feel compelled to share it here, perhaps for your benefit as well.

He told me, just a few months after He saved me, that any intake of alcohol in my life would replace the joy of the Holy Spirit that He wanted to give to me. His voice was clear; I had no other influence or voice in my life on this subject.

Prior to meeting the Lord, I was a "social drinker." I personally know the damage that even moderate drinking will do, and I have witnessed the destruction of relationships and lives due to the influence of alcohol.

Having said all of that, *I do not let* disagreements on this subject overrule the wonderful relationships I have with many precious brothers and sisters who do disagree with me. This issue is important to me but it may not be for them. We simply respect one another's opinions and preferences. I never wish to make anyone feel condemned or even argumentative on this matter; it is not worth it. I will not argue this subject because it is not worth the strife and division it could cause. I just state my testimony here for those who may be seekers. Ask God to speak to you about this subject.

So why did Jesus make wine? *See endnote.*[i]

God is Holy! If you wish to partake in the benefits of the covenant then be holy, be like He is! Treat His earthly Body properly. Don't criticize and gossip. Don't talk negatively, don't harbor ungodly thoughts rather take them to the Cross. Submit to your proper authorities, tithe, give to the poor, be unselfish, love your enemies, live a life of love, and don't judge others. When you don't live up to the pattern, then judge yourself, confess your sin, and Jesus will cleanse you. Be very prayerful about what you put into your body. If you want to change, ask Jesus to baptize you in His Holy Spirit and fire!

Remember who God is. Jesus made it clear that we partake of the covenant by His Words. Read this Scripture again and let it soak in.

John 6:53-56 says,

53 "Then Jesus said to them, 'Most assuredly, I say to you, unless you eat the flesh of the Son of Man and drink His blood, you have no life in you.

54 Whoever eats My flesh and drinks My blood has eternal life, and I will raise him up at the last day.

55 For My flesh is food indeed, and My blood is drink indeed.

56 He who eats My flesh and drinks My blood abides in Me, and I in him.'"

John 6:63 says,

63 "It is the Spirit who gives life; the flesh profits nothing. The words that I speak to you are spirit, and they *are life."*

Trust God's Word, it is His covenant transfer agent to you. Heaven and earth may pass away but His Word will stand forever! The reason many Christians cannot trust God's Word is that they cannot trust their own words. They are by nature disloyal people and liars. If that is you, don't fret, just get honest and repent. God will honor your honesty and repentance.

Use this checklist to see if there are areas of your life that are enslaved and that do not line up with love, with the nature of the Holy Spirit Who dwells in you.
Jesus gives us the victory as a done deal! Our faith in His Word is what will deliver us. We need to sharpen our relationship skills with Jesus, speaking the truth to Him, listening to His Word, the Holy Spirit and fellowshipping with the Church.

God's view of your slavery.
God was not caught off guard, neither was He indifferent to the Hebrew's slavery in Egypt. He heard their cry and felt their pain, as He hears and feels yours as well.

Exodus 2:23-25 says,

23 Now it happened in the process of time that the king of Egypt died. Then the children of Israel groaned because of the bondage, and they cried out; and their cry came up to God because of the bondage.

24 So God heard their groaning, and God remembered His covenant with Abraham, with Isaac, and with Jacob.

25 And God looked upon the children of Israel, and God acknowledged them."

Exodus 3:7-10 says,

7 "And the LORD said: 'I have surely seen the oppression of My people who are in Egypt, and have heard their cry because of their taskmasters, for I know their sorrows.

8 So I have come down to deliver them out of the hand of the Egyptians, and to bring them up from that land to a good and large land, to a land flowing with milk and honey, to the place of the Canaanites and the Hittites and the Amorites and the Perizzites and the Hivites and the Jebusites.

9 Now therefore, behold, the cry of the children of Israel has come to Me, and I have also seen the oppression with which the Egyptians oppress them.

10 Come now, therefore, and I will send you to Pharaoh that you may bring My people, the children of Israel, out of Egypt.'"

Notice that God remembered His blood covenant! This is key. His people may be living in something less than the blood covenant exchange and blessings, but God is not inactive. He remembers the blood that was shed in the ditch with Abram back in Genesis chapter 15. He remembers that He agreed to take the exchange of whatever Abram and his descendants would suffer.

God's redemption.

Isaiah chapter 61 was Jesus' mission statement in prophecy hundreds of years before His birth. It has to do with freeing slaves to receive their blood covenant blessing. The blessings actually include the entire chapter of Isaiah 61, but the following are just the first few verses.

Isaiah 61:1-3 says,

1 "The Spirit of the Lord GOD is upon Me, because the LORD has anointed Me to preach good tidings to the poor; He has sent Me to heal the brokenhearted, to proclaim liberty to the captives, and the opening of the prison to those who are bound;

2 To proclaim the acceptable year of the LORD, and the day of vengeance of our God; to comfort all who mourn,

3 To console those who mourn in Zion, to give them beauty for ashes, the oil of joy for mourning, the garment of praise for the spirit of heaviness; that they may be called trees of righteousness, the planting of the LORD, that He may be glorified.

John 8:31-36 says,

31 "Then Jesus said to those Jews who believed Him, 'If you abide in My word, you are My disciples indeed.

32 And you shall know the truth, and the truth shall make you free.'

33 They answered Him, 'We are Abraham's descendants, and have never been in bondage to anyone. How can you say, 'You will be made free?'

34 Jesus answered them, 'Most assuredly, I say to you, whoever commits sin is a slave of sin.

35 And a slave does not abide in the house forever, but a son abides forever.

36 Therefore if the Son makes you free, you shall be free indeed.'"

Notice, Jesus spoke this to the Jews "who had believed on him." They did not want to hear that they were slaves and that they needed someone to set them free. So many Christians today are the same way.

Paul tells us in Romans chapter 6 that we have "already" been set free from sin's slavery.

Romans 6:16-18 (NIV) says,

16 "Don't you know that when you offer yourselves to someone to obey him as slaves, you are slaves to the one whom you obey – whether you are slaves to sin, which leads to death, or to obedience, which leads to righteousness?

17 But thank be to God that, though you used to be slaves to sin, you wholeheartedly obeyed the form of teaching to which you were entrusted.

18 You have been set free from sin and have become slaves to righteousness."

He warns us in Romans chapter 6 that our choices can keep us in bondages.

It is true that we have been (past tense) set free. It is also true that we need to be (future tense) set free. Legally we are no longer slaves to sin and Satan once we make Jesus our Lord. However, there is a progressive realization of that fact. Progressively, we work out that truth in our lives. We must cooperate with God in His Day of Vengeance.

How can we cooperate to be free?

1. Stay in the Word of God and allow God access to your mind and soul.
2. Do not be content with ungodly behavior. Utilize the Word and the character of Jesus as a mirror so that you are not harboring a mindset or behavior that keeps you in bondage.
3. Study the grace of God verses "works" in the Bible and Bible lessons. Works should always be the result of grace received. God will deliver you from your slavery by His wonderful love and grace.
4. When you appreciate His love and grace your slavery will seem like it really is, horrible and something that you detest.
5. Offer yourself as a "slave" to Jesus. You cannot be owned by more than one.

Exodus 21:2,5-6 says,

"2 "If you buy a Hebrew servant, he shall serve six years; and in the seventh he shall go out free and pay nothing.
5 "But if the servant plainly says, 'I love my master, my wife, and my children; I will not go out free,'
6 "then his master shall bring him to the judges. He shall also bring him to the door, or to the doorpost, and his master shall pierce his ear with an awl; and he shall serve him forever."

Consider this.

You are the King's child asleep in your bedroom in the palace of your Daddy the King.

Suddenly you hear a voice at the window---
"You are not the Kings child. You are just pretending, You are my slave. You worry all the time about how you are going to buy food and clothes. You are addicted to .... You are just playing religious games," the voice says.

So you believe the voice and stay as a slave.

Suddenly your Daddy knocks at the door and says hear My voice son (daughter). Grace, grace be unto you. You are not a slave but My life lives in you as My child. I love you. Listen to My voice not the voice of the previous slave master. My Son purchased you at the slave auction years ago. Don't you remember? You were being auctioned off and the crowd was bidding. But My Son bid the highest price; His Blood!

The blood of Jesus has made you a free person! Appropriate it.

Chapter 10
Who Is Your Uncircumcised Philistine?

The war for your thought life.

David referred to Goliath as an uncircumcised Philistine.

1 Samuel 17:36 says,

36 "Your servant has killed both lion and bear; and this uncircumcised Philistine will be like one of them, seeing he has defied the armies of the living God."

Why did God choose David to fight Goliath rather then some of his older brothers or even other Israelites who had military experience?

David had a personal knowledge of the Blood Covenant with God. He gained this knowledge through his intimate relationship with God.

Psalms 25:14 says,

"14 The secret of the LORD is with those who fear Him, And He will show them His covenant."

David, for the most part, feared God. Sure he made some horrible mistakes, but his fear of losing his intimacy with God always came back. That describes the fear of the Lord; the fear of losing the relationship.

The term *uncircumcised* indicates a lack of blood covenant with God.

As we study this event with David and Goliath and relate it to the blood covenant, we will focus on one of our primary "uncircumcised enemies," our thoughts. As you study this story, notice that Goliath was throwing "thought bombs" at the Israelites. He was producing fear and intimidation, while all the while Israel was in blood covenant with God. God was their warrior but they took Goliath's words and believed them.

One of the biggest struggles in our walk with the Lord is overcoming false thought and belief systems. In our old nature our minds controlled us. Now, in our regenerated nature our spirit is to be in control. We are to take our thoughts captive to the truth.

However, so often we succumb to our old unregenerated thoughts. We hear a false thought message, receive it as truth, welcome the resulting emotion, and act upon it. Then our act becomes a habit, and eventually our habit becomes a satanic stronghold. Soon we have become prisoners to the enemy.

I believe that if we continue to succumb to our old unregenerated thoughts, we may miss God's best plan for our lives, now and in eternity.

Our thought life is the target of the enemy.

In the last chapter we saw how the blood covenant dealt with spiritual slavery. Now we are going to see the blood covenant in action from a door that the enemy uses to put us in slavery, perhaps the biggest one, our thoughts. We are surrounded by spiritual beings, both angels that protect us and evil spirits that try to seduce us.

2 Corinthians 10:3-6 (Amplified Bible) says,

3 "For though we walk (live) in the flesh, we are not carrying on our warfare according to the flesh and using mere human weapons.

4 For the weapons of our warfare are not physical [weapons of flesh and blood], but they are mighty before God for the overthrow and destruction of strongholds,

5 [Inasmuch as we] refute arguments and theories and reasonings and every proud and lofty thing [high thing] that sets itself up against the [true] knowledge of God; and we lead every thought and purpose away captive into the obedience of Christ (the Messiah, the Anointed One) [The Word],

6 Being in readiness to punish every [insubordinate for his] disobedience, when your own submission and obedience [as a church] are fully secured and complete.”

Notice in the above Scripture, the weapons are to war against the thought life. Also notice that this Scripture refers to “*arguments*” which are imaginations and reasonings; they are thoughts that we obtain. It also refers to strongholds, which are thoughts that have become demonic fortresses. So many of these arguments and strongholds can be a result of our past life. But also notice that this Scripture refers to “high things.” *High things* are thoughts that have been originated by satanic beings, they are fiery darts aimed at our minds. The enemy wants us to take the thought, act upon it until it becomes a habit, and then he sits back until he can make it a stronghold.

A stronghold is a fortress of false knowledge that is believed on as truth.

When a thought hits a stronghold, it immediately picks up the lie that the stronghold is harboring. It is almost like you don’t even have time to process the thought. The stronghold prevents, or at least tries to prevent, the thought from entering our system to chose to accept the thought or to decline it.

Our weapons are to protect our covenant rights of our “knowing” Him.

Notice in the Scripture quoted above from 2 Corinthians 10 that this warfare is against knowing God, or being intimate with Him, “...That sets itself up against the [true] knowledge of God” (v.5)

Knowing God is everything. *Knowing* is a word that suggests the most intimate personal contact, more than intellectual knowledge, but a close personal knowing. But we are in a war for that. The war is in and for our mind. Our greatest task is taking our thoughts captive with the weapons God has given us. Jesus has already defeated Satan at the Cross. He has already given us a complete blood covenant. Our war is not to defeat Satan, but simply to defend what our rightful inheritance is. Furthermore, Jesus is the mediator of the blood covenant. He is there to make sure that we receive the blood covenant privileges. But remember, His name is The Word.

I believe one of our problems believing in this intimacy with God is that we really have a hard time realizing how much God really loves us. I cannot answer that question, but I suggest that you ask Him to show at least a glimpse of His love. That should be enough to cause you to believe!

Ephesians 4:17 says,

17 "This I say, therefore, and testify in the Lord, that you should no longer walk as the rest of the Gentiles walk, in the futility of their mind."

When you are "knowing" Jesus, present tense, you make Him alive here on earth and the devil's plans are thwarted. This life is a war, and if we do not "know" Jesus on a daily basis, we will become discouraged. But the Apostle Paul showed us how he kept from becoming discouraged even when he was in what we would consider impossible circumstances.

2 Corinthians 4:16-18 (ISV) says,

" That's why we are not discouraged. No, even if outwardly we are wearing out, inwardly we are being renewed each and every day. This light, temporary nature of our suffering is producing for us an everlasting weight of glory, far beyond any comparison, because we do not look for things that can be seen but for things that cannot be seen. For things that can be seen are temporary, but things that cannot be seen are eternal.

The only way you can keep from being discouraged in this world is to do what Paul said, "we are being renewed each and every day." That renewal includes looking at the invisible, not only here on earth but also for that Day in Heaven.

That can only come by knowing Him. I believe that if we are renewed every day by feeding on Jesus that the voice of the satanic enemies will get drowned out. I believe that God's purpose for our lives will take place while on this earth, and that we will receive a wonderful reward on that Day that we see Him face to face.

Knowing Him! The New Blood Covenant is about knowing Him.

The removal of sin is what allows us to know Him. Jeremiah prophesied it.

Jeremiah 24:7 says,

7 "Then I will give them a heart to know Me, that I am the LORD; and they shall be My people, and I will be their God, for they shall return to Me with their whole heart."

Jeremiah 31:34 says,

34 "No more shall every man teach his neighbor, and every man his brother, saying, 'Know the LORD,' for they all shall know Me, from the least of them to the greatest of them, says the LORD. For I will forgive their iniquity, and their sin I will remember no more."

It is confirmed in the New Testament.

Hebrews 8:10-13 says,

10 For this is the covenant that I will make with the house of Israel after those days, says the LORD: I will put My laws in their mind and write them on their hearts; and I will be their God, and they shall be My people.

11 None of them shall teach his neighbor, and none his brother, saying, 'Know the LORD,' for all shall know Me, from the least of them to the greatest of them.

12 For I will be merciful to their unrighteousness, and their sins and their lawless deeds I will remember no more.'

13 In that He says, 'A new covenant,' He has made the first obsolete. Now what is becoming obsolete and growing old is ready to vanish away."

Examples of damaging thoughts.

Satan shoots thought bombs at us which lie about the character of God, against who we are in Christ, and which tempt us to speak negatively against our neighbors.

Perhaps some thoughts such as these will come. "Shame on you, you are not good enough for God to move on your behalf. You have been too bad." "God is too busy for you, you will have to make this one on your own." "Did God really mean that 'By His stripes you were healed.'" "It is okay; God understands your ungodly habit. He understands your heart, so it is okay just to keep on and not repent." "I am just an ordinary person, a sinner, saved by grace and going to Heaven." "I can never be as good as those other people, I can never succeed like they do." These are just a few. You need to judge your thoughts by the Word of God. Remember, Satan inspired Eve to take his thoughts and doubt the Word of God.

The seed of negative thoughts often can come from a broken past.

Anger, fear, shame, rejection, poor self-esteem, helplessness, hopelessness, discouragement, and loneliness can all produce and/or be the result of negative belief systems, emotions, actions and strongholds. Many times we fall into these negative belief systems due to dysfunctional and/or broken relationships in our lives. If you have come from families or lifestyles that have had broken relationships, especially with the father, and/or if your forefathers have experienced broken relationships and living for the world, then your belief system will default to "wrong."

So many people attempt to "medicate" these feelings and emotions with the wrong prescription. Most often these are caused by some broken connection in your past. Perhaps they are caused by a bad or a non-existing relationship with your father. Maybe you have suffered rejection from loved ones or peers. It could even be from a generational curse coming down your family line that is just now popping its head up and you cannot figure out what happened!

How do we deal with negative and destructive thought patterns within the blood covenant?

Most of us have heard the David and Goliath story. Let us look at it again from the point of view of deliverance from our bondages that result from an undisciplined thought life.

Israel had been disobedient to God on an "on and off" basis. Saul was king. The Philistines were intimidating God's people and they were afraid, even Saul was afraid.

In view of all of this there was at least one, little David the sheepherder, who understood something about the blood. He must have learned, at least in part, about the hand of the covenant God out in the field when he killed the lion and the bear. Most likely he killed them with his sling and a stone. That is no small feat. However, David had a way of hearing God and responding to Him (Psalm 23, 32, 51). We know that faith comes by hearing God speak. David had faith in the blood covenant with God. Let us take a lesson from David to slay our own Goliaths.

Remember, Israel had a blood covenant with God that promised that He would defeat their enemies. Their false belief system gave Goliath the door to curse them and instill fear.

David refused to use the arm of the flesh, Saul's amour. Saul represents the old nature, our flesh, our unregenerated "king." One's armor also represents a covenant item. When two enter into a blood covenant, they exchange armor. Most often we do not really turn our backs on the strength of our old flesh nature until we see it fail us. But David somehow knew that he already had Other Armor.

1 Samuel 17:38-39 says,

> *38 "So Saul clothed David with his armor, and he put a bronze helmet on his head; he also clothed him with a coat of mail.*
>
> *39 David fastened his sword to his armor and tried to walk, for he had not tested them. And David said to Saul, 'I cannot walk with these, for I have not tested them.' So David took them off."*

David refused to be intimidated by Satan, Goliath. I can guarantee you that Satan is active, alive and he is not without his plans to keep you in slavery and bondage!

1 Samuel 17:46-47 says,

46 "This day the LORD will deliver you into my hand, and I will strike you and take your head from you. And this day I will give the carcasses of the camp of the Philistines to the birds of the air and the wild beasts of the earth, that all the earth may know that there is a God in Israel.

47 Then all this assembly shall know that the LORD does not save with sword and spear; for the battle is the LORD'S, and He will give you into our hands."

David refused to be discouraged by his own family, Eliab his brother. People within our families, and even the Body of Christ, may discourage us. These people who should be our cheerleaders, but due to their own bondages they attempt to bring us down to their level with discouragement.

1 Samuel 17:28 says,

28 "Now Eliab his oldest brother heard when he spoke to the men; and Eliab's anger was aroused against David, and he said, 'Why did you come down here? And with whom have you left those few sheep in the wilderness? I know your pride and the insolence of your heart, for you have come down to see the battle.'"

David trusted in the Word of God, in the covenant of blood.

How do we know that? He expressed his faith in the blood when he cried out in 1 Samuel 17:36 said, "Your servant has killed both lion and bear; and this uncircumcised Philistine will be like one of them, seeing he has defied the armies of the living God."

1 Samuel 17:45-46 says,

45 "Then David said to the Philistine, 'You come to me with a sword, with a spear, and with a javelin. But I come to you in the name of the LORD of hosts, the God of the armies of Israel, whom you have defied.

46 This day the LORD will deliver you into my hand, and I will strike you and take your head from you. And this day I will give the carcasses of the camp of the Philistines to the birds of the air and the wild beasts of the earth, that all the earth may know that there is a God in Israel.

47 Then all this assembly shall know that the LORD does not save with sword and spear; for the battle is the LORD'S, and He will give you into our hands.'"

David had the "name" of God. He knew that God had given His name in blood covenant to Israel, and David understood the significance. He knew that Goliath the Philistine did not have a covenant with God. The Philistines, in many respects, were better warriors, better cultured and stronger people. But that made no difference to David. He understood the value of the blood exchange, the blood covenant!

David used five smooth stones and his sling.

1 Samuel 17:40 says,

40 "Then he took his staff in his hand; and he chose for himself five smooth stones..."

Five is the number for grace. Rocks and stones often refer to the Word. The Word of grace perhaps represents David's choice of five smooth stones. Christ is often referred to metaphorically as the stone or the rock.

David, unlike his brothers, had a personal relationship with God, which he developed while in the wilderness tending the sheep. He is the one who wrote Psalm 23. Certainly during his conversations with God, David learned about the blood covenant. Notice how David takes control of his thoughts in full view of potential danger and negative circumstances. David was speaking the Word of faith; he was slinging smooth stones at his thoughts.

Psalm 23:1-6 (KJV) says,

1 "The LORD is my shepherd; I shall not want.
2 He maketh me to lie down in green pastures: he leadeth me beside the still waters.
3 He restoreth my soul: he leadeth me in the paths of righteousness for his name's sake.
4 Yea, though I walk through the valley of the shadow of death, I will fear no evil: for thou art with me; thy rod and thy staff they comfort me.
5 Thou preparest a table before me in the presence of mine enemies: thou anointest my head with oil; my cup runneth over.
6 Surely goodness and mercy shall follow me all the days of my life: and I will dwell in the house of the LORD for ever."

David perhaps chose smooth stones, ones that had been through years of polishing in the river, because they were aerodynamic and would hit their mark with accuracy. Our polished stones are those Scriptures that God has made real to us, those that have been polished in our meditation, memorization and study. We need to "polish" some stones, some of the Word, so that we may have our "smooth stones of grace" with which to fell our giant, demonic and negative thoughts.

Now you take the Word, your smooth stone, put it into the sling of your mouth, and speak it to your Goliath every time your thoughts begin to attempt to take over your life in a negative way.

Take your every thought captive. As they come up, give them to God intentionally. But first, forgive those who may have originated your problem, forgive those discourage who you, and turn your back on your own fleshly power. Then watch your stone hit the giant and fell him. Then take the sword of the Spirit and cut Goliath's head off!

In summary:

Jesus gave us the Blood Covenant that removes our sin. One of the main benefits of that is that we may have a knowing of Him, intimately- real time contact. When we are in the present tense of knowing Him, His power works in us, for us and for others in the world. Satan knows that our thought life can keep us from the power of God; therefore that is where he concentrates his "big guns."

What are some warfare disciplines?
Ask God to reveal any strongholds and/or false thoughts that you have believed. Like "Your child will never be saved," or "You will never have enough money to make life work."
Keep your mind stayed on the Word of God. Meditate on the Word. Keep a habit an honest confession pouring out your heart to the Lord. Keep the Word coming out of your mouth. Practice a life of praise, worship and thanksgiving. Repentance from an ungodly lifestyle or habit will lift the veil of our misunderstanding of the Word of God, and will make the Word alive to your mind and heart (2 Corinthians 3:16).

The armor of God is in Ephesians chapter 6.

1. **Stand against the devil. This means to protect your position of victory.**
2. **Gird your waist with truth.** Truth and integrity in your lifestyle. *See comment below.*
3. **Breastplate of righteousness.** Knowing our righteousness and who we are in Him. Continually studying and confirming that issue.
4. **Shod your feed with the preparation of the Gospel of peace.**
5. **Above all take up the shield of faith to quench the fiery darts.** Faith comes by hearing the Word.
6. **Helmet of salvation.** This is to protect your mind.
7. **The sword of the Spirit, the Word of God.**
8. **Praying always in the spirit,** being watchful with perseverance and supplication. Praying for extended periods

of time in the Holy Spirit is very powerful. It will bring supernatural results into your life!! *See comment below.*

I can just hear Jesus saying,
"I took My thoughts captive for you. Will you do the same for Me?" Now, follow the path of David to break your old unregenerated thought pattern. Become a covenant thinker!
David refused to be intimidated by Satan, Goliath.
David refused to be discouraged by his own family, Eliab his brother.
David trusted in the Word of God, in the covenant of blood.
David had the "name" of God.
David used five smooth stones and his sling. Five is the number for grace.
Read the story of David and Goliath from 1 Samuel 17:1-58.

Warning about truth! 2 Thessalonians 2:9-12 says,

"9 The coming of the lawless one is according to the working of Satan, with all power, signs, and lying wonders,

10 and with all unrighteous deception among those who perish, because they did not receive the love of the truth, that they might be saved.

11 And for this reason God will send them strong delusion, that they should believe the lie,

12 that they all may be condemned who did not believe the truth but had pleasure in unrighteousness."

God sends the love of the truth to every human being, however not every human being receives the love of the truth. Like a football that is thrown is not always received. When one does not receive it then God sends a strong delusion to believe lies.

So it is with the warfare to protect your mind against demons. If you do not receive the love of the truth, you will be deceived by the thoughts that demons send to you. I personally know Christians who are in this position.

The weapons of our warfare are designed to keep our relationship (knowing) with God. After recognizing the important defensive weapons in Ephesians chapter 6, don't forget the most powerful weapon of all, The Word, Jesus, spoken into this atmosphere! What could be more powerful? When we speak The Word out loud, Jesus is being released in ways that we cannot comprehend. His Word seizes the environment!

John 1:1-5, 13-14-14 says,

"1 In the beginning was the Word, and the Word was with God, and the Word was God.

2 He was in the beginning with God.

3 All things were made through Him, and without Him nothing was made that was made.

4 In Him was life, and the life was the light of men.

5 And the light shines in the darkness, and the darkness did not comprehend it.

13 who were born, not of blood, nor of the will of the flesh, nor of the will of man, but of God.

14 And the Word became flesh and dwelt among us, and we beheld His glory, the glory as of the only begotten of the Father, full of grace and truth."

Chapter 11
From Lo Debar to Jerusalem

2 Samuel chapter 9 records a very interesting story of King David rescuing Jonathon's son Mephibosheth according to the commitment of a blood covenant. This story demonstrates some very important truths of the Cross of Jesus Christ. Mephibosheth was living in Lo Debar, which means a place of no bread. Jesus is the bread of life. The Word is our bread. Lo Debar to us is the place of no Word. In the story, Mephibosheth lived in Lo Debar. He was withering away because he had no Word, even in view of the fact that he was the lawful recipient of a blood covenant with a king.

Who was Mephibosheth?
It all started with the tremendous godly love between David and Jonathan. Jonathan was King Saul's son. Saul was jealous of David who had been anointed king. Saul was trying to kill David. In spite of this tension, David and Jonathan had a strong respect and a deep love for one another. I don't think that we can even compare it to something in our lives today, because they had a different culture then.

Jonathan, Mephibosheth's father, had made a covenant with David.

1 Samuel 18:1-4 (KJV) says,

1 "And it came to pass, when he had made an end of speaking unto Saul, that the soul of Jonathan was knit with the soul of David, and Jonathan loved him as his own soul. Then Jonathan and David made a covenant, because he loved him as his own soul.

2 And Saul took him [David] that day, and would let him go no more home to his father's house.

3 Then Jonathan and David made a covenant, because he loved him as his own soul.

4 And Jonathan stripped himself of the robe that was upon him, and gave it to David, and his garments, even to his sword, and to his bow, and to his girdle."

Most people do not understand the truths about covenants, especially blood covenants.

It is the strongest relationship that exists and it carries the most responsibility! Also, most people do not relate the blood covenant to the Word of God and to our relationship with God.

David blessed Mephibosheth out of covenant love.

The word for covenant love is checed. Checed, a Hebrew word, means covenant love. In Greek the same word for covenant love is agape. The Old Testament gives checed a very weak translation, usually calling it loving **kindness** or mercy. It can only be described in terms of a blood covenant.

David was an example of the heart of God showing that He has an ache to bless His covenant people. David was a callused warrior, but he cried out to bless his blood covenant family.

The following is some historic background about the war between the Philistines and the divided kingdoms, Israel and Judah.

As recorded in 1st and 2nd Samuel, during the time of Saul, Jonathon and David, there was an intense war going on between Israel and the Philistines. During that time Saul was intense on killing David. David refused to harm Saul even though he had opportunities, maybe out of respect for the office of the king and perhaps because David had cut a covenant with Jonathon, Saul's son. In 2 Samuel chapter 1 David learned about the death of Saul and Jonathan during the war.

David took over as king over Judah but Saul's family kept control over Israel. There are records of wars between the two kingdoms. Eventually David was made king over both kingdoms.

It is with this bloody background that fear hit the house where Mephibosheth was living and the nurse dropped him and made him crippled for life.

Fear of David caused the accident. But David had no intention of hurting them. David actually mourned for Abner, and

Saul (2 Samuel 3:33). This was the heart of checed, covenant love.

Even after this horrible background, King David cried out to bless someone in Saul's household.

Can you imagine after all of the abuse David received from the house of Saul, that he now is aching to bless one of Saul's descendants? Notice in this Scripture that is aching to bless was for Jonathan's sake!

One day, the covenant love hit David so hard he could not stand it.

He just had to bless someone. So he called to find out who was a survivor of Saul's household, the father of Jonathan, with whom he had a covenant.

He sent for Mephibosheth to tell him of his love. Jesus is sending for us to tell us of His love, and He is sending us to tell others of His love for them. I can only imagine the entourage that the king must have sent for Mephibosheth. I can only imagine what fear Mephibosheth must have felt when he saw all of the army and weaponry of Israel at his front door.

2 Samuel 9:1-13 (NIV) says,

*1 "David asked, 'Is there anyone still left of the house of Saul to whom I can show **kindness for Jonathan's sake?'***

2 Now there was a servant of Saul's household named Ziba. They called him to appear before David, and the king said to him, 'Are you Ziba?' 'Your servant,' he replied.

*3 The king asked, 'Is there no-one still left of the house of Saul to whom I can show God's **kindness**?' Ziba answered the king, 'There is still a son of Jonathan; he is crippled in both feet.'*

*4 'Where is he?' the king asked. Ziba answered, 'He is at the house of **Makir** son of **Ammiel** in Lo Debar.'*

5 So King David had him brought from Lo Debar, from the house of Makir son of Ammiel.

6 When Mephibosheth son of Jonathan, the son of Saul, came to David, he bowed down to pay him honour. David said, 'Mephibosheth!' 'Your servant,' he replied.

[Makir means salesman, a merchandiser, as if to sell a daughter into a marriage of slavery. Ammiel means a clan of the people of God. Put them together and we see that we can be people of God who are sold into the slavery. This is Lo Debar, the place of no supplies, no bread of God. This has made us slaves to Satan even though we are children of God.]

7 "'Don't be afraid,' David said to him, 'for I will surely show you ***kindness*** *for the sake of your father Jonathan. I will restore to you all the land that belonged to your grandfather Saul,* ***and you will always eat at my table****.'*

8 Mephibosheth bowed down and said, 'What is your servant, that you should notice a dead dog like me?'

9 Then the king summoned Ziba, Saul's servant, and said to him, 'I have given your master's grandson everything that belonged to Saul and his family.

10 You and your sons and your servants are to farm the land for him and bring in the crops, so that your master's grandson may be provided for. And Mephibosheth, grandson of your master, ***will always eat at my table****.' (Now Ziba had fifteen sons and twenty servants.)*

11 Then Ziba said to the king, 'Your servant will do whatever my lord the king commands his servant to do.' So Mephibosheth ate at David's table like one of the king's sons.

12 Mephibosheth had a young son named Mica, and all the members of Ziba's household were servants of Mephibosheth.

13 And Mephibosheth lived in Jerusalem, because he always ate at the king's table, and he was crippled in both feet."

That was the cry of David, but it is also the cry of Jesus.

Ephesians 2:4 (Amplified Bible) says,

4 But God—so rich is He in His mercy! Because of and in order to ***satisfy the great and wonderful and intense love with which He loved us,***

5 Even when we were dead (slain) by [our own] shortcomings and trespasses, He made us alive together in fellowship and in union with Christ; [He gave us the very life of Christ Himself, the same new life with which He quickened Him, for] it is by grace (His favor and mercy which you did not deserve) that you are saved (delivered from judgment and made partakers of Christ's salvation).

6 And He raised us up together with Him and made us sit down together [giving us joint seating with Him] in the heavenly sphere [by virtue of our being] in Christ Jesus (the Messiah, the Anointed One).

Mephibosheth's disability is a picture of our spiritual disability. His name means a dispeller of confusion and shame; one that scatters and breaks into pieces. Apparently God was using this name to indicate that when one finally gets to Jerusalem and understands that he has a blood covenant with the King, all the shame of the past is dispelled and broken into small pieces and cast out forever. Shame is a killer because it lies against who God made you to be. Shame attacks your very being and says that you will never be worthy or any good. You may have done some terrible things, which brings guilt, but God is not casting shame on you. He says to you that you are His, that you are righteous and His son/daughter.

Remember, Mephibosheth was Jonathan's son, the grandson of Saul, who had tried to kill David. He had been living beneath his rights. He had a covenant with the king and did not know it. He was living in Lo Debar, which means a place of no bread. He was actually living in fear of David, the king of Judah and Israel. His maid dropped him when he was young as the family was fleeing. They thought that they were fleeing the wrath of David.

However they were mistaken.

David made sure that Mephibosheth was served the rest of his life by Ziba and his family. They ran the farm for Mephibosheth. David already had possession of Saul's wealth; the rest of Saul's family had pretty much melted into the desert. David could have kept this wealth, but he chose to exercise his covenant love, his checed.

David exercised all of his kingly authority for this covenant, and Mephibosheth ate at David's table the rest of his life.

Did Mephibosheth deserve this? Why do we need a blood covenant with a king?

Since the beginning of creation, man was the subject of blood covenants. Adam had a covenant with God that he broke. Many primitive cultures still believe that blood covenant brothers are closer relatives than those born of the same mother. A blood covenant intermingles the life of both partners and creates a new common life.

The King's Table

> *7 "'Don't be afraid,' David said to him, 'for I will surely show you* ***kindness*** *for the sake of your father Jonathan. I will restore to you all the land that belonged to your grandfather Saul, and you will always eat at my table.'*

What do we eat at our King's Table?

First we are fed on being in the presence of the Creator of all things, the Eternal I AM, the God who was never created, who always was!

Our greatest reward is to be in close intimate fellowship with the King, a deep often quiet communion with the One who loves us more than we can imagine. The longing for this is inherited by us from the King Himself who longs just to be with us quietly enjoying one another. Mephibosheth had not been seeking the King, but the King sought him.

When we experience this our needs for deliverance and material supplies take second place and pale in comparison with the rewards of knowing that we are no longer subjects of the King, but his child. We sense His deep love for us and His seeking us for His own enjoyment.

Then we are fed the Word of God planted in a human heart as a seed.

The Word of God is the Bread of Life. See next chapter for how the Word provides for all of your temporal needs while you are on earth,

Some comments about kindness.

Notice how many times David was motivated by kindness. I have heard and believe that one of the primary differences between animals and humans is the potential to be kind. I have witnessed wild animals in South Africa and how they hunt and destroy one another. I have seen right here in my own church how so many humans do not use kindness and destroy each other. I have been convicted by God how I also have, on some occasions, not shown kindness. Like in Matthew 7:3-5, the log in your eye compared to the splinter in your brother's eye. Mephibosheth was living in shame. Kindness is one of the anti-shame medications.

So many people, even Christians in church, instead of being kind judge one another, point out their faults and remind them of the burdens that may have. Then they give them advice on how to stop sinning so their burdens, sufferings, or sicknesses can be relieved. We are healed by love and kindness. Mephibosheth was healed because of David's kindness.

We need to "dress properly."

Colossians 3:12-15 says,

"12 Therefore, as the elect of God, holy and beloved, put on tender mercies, kindness, humility, meekness, longsuffering;

13 bearing with one another, and forgiving one another, if anyone has a complaint against another; even as Christ forgave you, so you also must do.

14 But above all these things put on love, which is the bond of perfection.

15 And let the peace of God rule in your hearts, to which also you were called in one body; and be thankful."

Mephibosheth's last days. The gift or the giver?
2 Samuel Chapter 16:1-4 reveals the story of how Ziba, Mephibosheth's servant successfully attempted to steal his inheritance, the entire estate that belonged to Saul, his grandfather. Ziba lied to David about Mephibosheth, accusing him of attempting to take the king's throne from David.

David went along with it for a while until he encountered Mephibosheth personally as told in 2 Samuel 19:24-30. The record was set straight and the lie that Ziba told was revealed. David, in an effort to restore the inheritance to Mephibosheth, declared that Saul's estate be divided between Mephibosheth and Ziba. Mephibosheth answered with a most remarkable statement. He told David to let Ziba have the entire inheritance, and that all he wanted was to be with David. He was just happy that David had survived and that being with him and eating at his table would be enough.

!

Chapter 12
The King's Table

Remember from the previous chapter that Mephibosheth had been invited to dine at the King's Table, King David's, because of a blood covenant that flowed down to Mephibosheth from his father Jonathan.

> **2 Samuel 9:7 says,** *"'Don't be afraid,' David said to him [Mephibosheth], 'for I will surely show you kindness for the sake of your father Jonathan. I will restore to you all the land that belonged to your grandfather Saul, and you will always eat at my table.'*

What do we eat at our King's Table?

First we are fed on being in the presence of the Creator of all things, the Eternal I AM, the God who was never created, who always was!

Our greatest reward is to be in close intimate fellowship with the King, a deep often quiet communion with the One who loves us more than we can imagine. The longing for this is inherited by us from the King Himself who longs just to be with us quietly enjoying one another. Mephibosheth had not been seeking the King, but the King sought him.

When we experience this our needs for deliverance and material supplies take second place and pale in comparison with the rewards of knowing that we are no longer subjects of the King, but his child. We sense His deep love for us and His seeking us for His own enjoyment.

Then we are fed the Word of God planted in a human heart as a seed.

The Word of God is the Bread of Life.

Matthew 4:4 says,

> *4 "But He answered and said, 'It is written, 'Man shall not live [sustain their very life] by bread alone, but by every word that proceeds from the mouth of God.'"*

If we don't allow the Word to be planted in our hearts as a seed we are living in Lo Debar, and we are trying to make life work in our own power and operating in the Kingdom of this World system instead of the Kingdom of God.

Jesus connected the Word with His covenant love.

John 6:50-51 says,

50 "This is the bread which comes down from heaven, that one may eat of it and not die.

51 I am the living bread which came down from heaven. If anyone eats of this bread, he will live forever; and the bread that I shall give is My flesh, which I shall give for the life of the world."

John 6:63 says,

63 "It is the Spirit who gives life; the flesh profits nothing. The words that I speak to you are spirit, and they are life."

In verse 6:63, He said that His Word is His flesh and blood, the transmitter of the covenant. Jesus made it clear that the Word was the main issue. Words are the only medium that transfers life between the spirit and natural realm.

Jesus told the poor people in this chapter that they needed a cure for their curse of poverty. They needed to eat His flesh and drink His blood. Then He made the transition to the spiritual. He said the flesh profits nothing, but His Words are spirit and they are life. Read the story in John 6.

Jesus is aching to bless you and me with His covenant love. His primary method of transferring His life, His blood, His blessings, is through His Word. He does not just dispense blessings like in a cafeteria line; today I need funds, next week I need healing, etc. No. He dispenses Himself, His very life; that is the blessing! He does that through His Word anointed by the Holy Spirit. He reserves His blessings for the simple, the childlike, the desperate (like Mephibosheth), and hides them from the proud and religious intellectual people.

The seed of the Word in your heart is God's method for

supplying your temporal needs.
God delivers everything we need to make it in this life and everything we need to develop godly character by giving us His seed promises in the Word. Then we stand on that Word until its own power does the work. That is blood covenant! That is His power and not ours! That is grace!

2 Peter 1:3-4 says,

3 "as His divine power has given to us all things that pertain to life and ***godliness****, through the knowledge of Him who called us by glory and virtue,*

4 by which have been given to us exceedingly great and precious promises, that through these you may be partakers of the divine nature, having escaped the corruption that is in the world through lust."

Notice in the above Scripture that we are promised all things that pertain to life and godliness. We are not to expect our temporal needs to be without interruption if godliness is not on the increase in our lives!

From Thorns to Fruit!

Adam had the privilege of living by fruit by the Word of God. When he departed from living by the Word from God, he was told by God that there would be no more fruit but instead he would work by the sweat of his brow and he would be under the curse of thorns. Jesus wore those thorns for us at the Cross.

Listen closely! This is a mystery that Jesus unveiled for us.

Mark 4:11 says,

11 "And He said to them, 'To you it has been given to know the ***mystery*** *of the kingdom of God; but to those who are outside, all things come in parables.'"*

Notice, He said the mystery, not a mystery.

Here is how you can move from Lo Debar to Jerusalem.

This parable in Mark chapter 4:1-20 is one of the most important passages in Scripture. It shows us how the Word of

God transfers covenant benefits to us.

Mark 4:1-14 says,

1 "And again He began to teach by the sea. And a great multitude was gathered to Him, so that He got into a boat and sat in it on the sea; and the whole multitude was on the land facing the sea.

2 Then He taught them many things by parables, and said to them in His teaching:

3 'Listen! Behold, a sower went out to sow.

4 And it happened, as he sowed, that some seed fell by the wayside; and the birds of the air came and devoured it.

5 Some fell on stony ground, where it did not have much earth; and immediately it sprang up because it had no depth of earth.

6 But when the sun was up it was scorched, and because it had no root it withered away.

7 And some seed fell among thorns; and the thorns grew up and choked it, and it yielded no crop.

8 But other seed fell on good ground and yielded a crop that sprang up, increased and produced: some thirtyfold, some sixty, and some a hundred.'

9 And He said to them, 'He who has ears to hear, let him hear!'

10 But when He was alone, those around Him with the twelve asked Him about the parable.

11 And He said to them, 'To you it has been given to know the mystery of the kingdom of God; but to those who are outside, all things come in parables,

12 so that 'Seeing they may see and not perceive, And hearing they may hear and not understand; Lest they should turn, And their sins be forgiven them.''

13 And He said to them, 'Do you not understand this parable? How then will you understand all the parables?

14 The sower sows the word. [The sower is God, through Jesus, the Word and the Holy Spirit, perhaps through the agency of man]."

As we practice intimacy with Jesus through prayer and His Word, He plants the Word-seed into the ground of our hearts, and His purposes are realized through us in the fruit bearing process.

What kind of fruit can we expect?

I submit from the Word and from experience the three types of fruit are:

1. Character, taken from the Law that is in the Ark.
2. Manna, or supplies for this life, taken from Manna that is in the Ark.
3. Ministry, taken from Aaron's Rod that is in the Ark.

God told David in Psalm 23 that he would sit at the King's Table in the presence of his enemies.

Psalms 23:5 says,

> *"5 You prepare a table before me in the presence of my enemies; You anoint my head with oil; My cup runs over."*

When you eat at the King's Table you will experience your spiritual enemies.

The Parable of the Sower in Mark 4 makes it clear that Satan will come immediately when the Word is sown in your heart.

Why? Because bearing fruit with God will not only provide for your needs but will also bringing in the Kingdom of God according to God's purpose for your realm of influence.

Satan is real!

His only real weapon is to steal the Word. He is a liar and deceiver. He knows that the Word defeated him, so he convinces people in general, and even Christians that they do not need to live on the Word of God. He portrays it as a rulebook, a guide to live by, something we are obligated to read in order to be good Christians. He hides the supernatural qualities of the Word.

The seed of the Word requires a good heart in order to bear fruit.

Tribulation and persecution will come after you receive the Word.

Satan attempts to make us think that we did not hear the Word. He makes us become ashamed of the Word through persecution. He tells us "See, the Word is not working." However if you know that this is the script of life, then you can endure. Tribulation of some sort will come into your life when you depend upon the Word! It will also test the condition of your heart.

Mark 4:15 says,

"15 **[heart condition number one, a hard heart]** *"And these are the ones by the wayside where the word is sown. When they hear, Satan comes immediately and takes away the word that was sown in their hearts."*

Mark 4:16-17 says,

16 **[heart condition number two, a shallow heart]** *"These likewise are the ones sown on stony ground who, when they hear the word, immediately receive it with gladness;*

17 and they have no root in themselves, and so endure only for a time. Afterward, when tribulation or persecution arises for the word's sake, immediately they stumble."

Mark 4:18-20 says,

18 **[heart condition number three, a worldly heart]** *"Now these are the ones sown among thorns; they are the ones who hear the word,*

19 and the cares of this world, the deceitfulness of riches, and the desires for other things entering in choke the word, and it becomes unfruitful.

20 **[heart condition number four, an honest heart]** *But these are the ones sown on good ground, those who hear the word, accept it, and bear fruit: some thirtyfold, some sixty, and some a hundred.'"*

This is the overcoming process.

It usually entails much pain. Seeds, even though silent, work with much violence.

Matthew 11:12 says,

12 "And from the days of John the Baptist until now the

kingdom of heaven suffers violence, and the violent take it by force."

The word violence has a Greek definition that infers the type of violence that occurs when something is growing. For instance, the roots of a tree can become violent to structure nearby.

God's amazing ways!

If you have decided to operate your life in the Kingdom of God while on this earth by allowing God to be your provider through the seed and fruit process, then you will for sure experience "fires" in your life.

It works like this:

1. The seed of the Word is planted in your heart by God.

2. Satan comes to steal the Word through the many ways described in Mark chapter 4. He knows that if you bear fruit that the Kingdom of God will replace a portion of his kingdom here on earth.

3. Satan's attacks are like "fires" in your life. But these fires actually prepare your heart, or the ground of the seed, to bear more fruit more quickly.

4. How? Fires often are very healthy for the ground. They can cause the new growth to grow quicker and healthier.

A quote from Leonard F. DeBano

http://forest.moscowfsl.wsu.edu/smp/solo/documents/GTRs/INT_280/DeBano_INT-280.php

> *Fire significantly affects soil properties because organic matter (OM) located on, or near, the soil surface is rapidly combusted. The changes in OM, in turn, affect several chemical, physical, and microbiological properties of the underlying soil. Although some nutrients are volatilized and lost, most nutrients are made more available. Fire acts as a rapid mineralizing agent (St. John and Rundel 1976) that releases nutrients instantaneously as contrasted to natural decomposition processes, which may require years or, in some cases, decades.*

5. As you go through these spiritual fires the Holy Spirit will show you areas in your life that need repentance. This process makes the ground more suitable for fruit, as your character is refined by fire.

6. The fruit blossoms! Not only are your needs met, but the Kingdom of God is expanded on this earth, and the demonic powers here on earth that attacked you are defeated.

If you are not trusting in God's Word to be planted in your heart, in order to supply your every need, you are living in Lo Debar. You need to move to Jerusalem! Now pack your bags and move from Lo Debar to Jerusalem. Ask God to plants His seeds in your heart for what He wants you to have and/or do. You will be blessed and be a blessing.

Mephibosheth refused all of the earthly inheritance that he had coming to him via his grandfather Saul, probably millions. All he wanted at the end of all his trials was to sit at King David's table. Kindness works!

Chapter 13

The Blood Covenant - Hope for Your Life

We all need hope and purpose for our lives. I know in my life that I had come to the end of all the plans and purposes that I could have imagined. I kept trying to discover why I was put here, and what God's reasoning was for creating me. After I had achieved one of my financial dreams at 30 years old, I felt emptier than ever, and cried out to a God that I had not yet met. I told Him that obviously He had created humans, just look at the genius of our bodies, our circulatory system, our brain, etc. I felt that if He created something so great, then how could humans just waste their lives on things that did not matter. He heard my cry, but waited eight more years to reveal Himself to me.

I heard a man tell me one time, "I can live without love, without faith, but I cannot live without hope." I think he had something to say.

What is hope? How does it relate to purpose in life? The Biblical meaning of hope is not anything like the common *hope* we often use, as in, "Oh, I hope this thing works out for me."

Biblical hope means the expectation of good, to anticipate with pleasure.

Hope is like the architectural drawings for a building yet to be built. It is the design, the vision of what cannot yet be seen. After the architect makes the drawings, or creates the vision, then the builder must add energy to create what the drawings say.

Another analogy is that hope is like the thermostat on your furnace; is the goal-setting device. You look at the thermometer and it shows that the house is only 50 degrees. You desire the temperature to be 70 degrees. Do you just look at it and complain? No. You turn the thermostat to 70 degrees and create the hope, or the vision. Now the furnace must be powerful enough to create the vision. If it is not, it does not matter how high you turn the thermostat.

We can create our own hope that is not God's plan for our

lives.

I used to create my own visions, as most of you probably have. The problem was that none of them were God's plan for my life. Some of them came about; those that my own power could perform. Many did not. Even those that came to pass were total disappointments because I did not know about God's vision, God's hope for me.

Galatians 6:7 says,

> *7 "Do not be deceived, God is not mocked; for whatever a man sows, that he will also reap."*

I had reaped some bad "stuff" because I had sown bad things. I was not living my vision or dream. I had become miserable, and felt powerless to change things.

When we create our own hope, we are sowing bad seeds for our lives; we are actually sowing sin. Not only do we sow bad seeds, but most likely our ancestors have sown bad seeds that we now reap due to the law of the generational curse.

Creating our own hope brings Satan on our case.

These are indeed bad seeds, but they potentially have more destructive power than one might think at first glance. Satan and his associates get a foothold, a legal right to perpetuate curses and destruction in our lives and in the lives of our children.

Jacob was in much the same condition in Genesis chapters 30-31.

If you have sown bad seeds in your life like Jacob did, and now you are reaping bad things into your life, hang on; the Blood Covenant will correct things.

We must reach the end of ourselves like Jacob did. Jacob had reaped what he had sown. He was on a detour from God's plan, but not in God's mind. When we are marked by God, He comes to us in our prisons made by bad choices and gives us a vision, a Word, to rescue us. Jacob was marked as a covenant man. God has a perfect plan for each covenant son or daughter of His. It is a predestined path; it is called "abundant life." It is customized for each one of us.

God intervened in Jacob's life with a vision, which set him free from the bondage, which was a result of his own sowing and reaping. The vision contained within itself the very power to perform that which God wanted for Jacob's life.

Ephesians 2:10 (Amplified Bible) says,

10 "For we are God's [own] handiwork (His workmanship), recreated in Christ Jesus, [born anew] that we may do those good works which God predestined (planned beforehand) for us [taking paths which He prepared ahead of time], that we should walk in them [living the good life which He prearranged and made ready for us to live]."

How does this work?

You might say that even if God gave you the hope, the vision for the future, that you don't have the power to pull it off. Good!

Here is how it works.

Hebrews 11:1-2 (Amplified Bible) says,

1 "NOW FAITH is the assurance (the confirmation, the title deed) of the things [we] hope for, being the proof of things [we] do not see and the conviction of their reality [faith perceiving as real fact what is not revealed to the senses].

2 For by [faith – trust and holy fervor born of faith] the men of old had divine testimony borne to them and obtained a good report."

1. Hope. Through your relationship with God in His Word, He will reveal the vision, the hope or architectural drawing that He has for your life. Later in this chapter I will go into more detail on how this works.

Romans 15:13 says,

13 "Now may the God of hope fill you with all joy and peace in believing, that you may abound in hope by the power of the Holy Spirit."

You may or may not know exactly what the vision represents. It may be a promise as precise as, "I will take care of your financial needs." It may be very vague, as is usually the case when your future is concerned. But you need to trust that He has a destined purpose for you that you may not be able to explain.

2. Faith. The seed that is planted in your heart has the ability to produce what the vision or the hope represents. The acorn has the power to produce an oak tree. The seed of corn has the ability to produce a new stalk of corn. I have been told, that if you were to cut open the acorn, you could see the picture of the oak tree it represents.

Having this Word come to you from God produces the faith that produces the title deed, (the ownership) to the hope, or the vision that God has for you.

3. Perseverance and obedience. The next step is to resist the doubt caused by the delay in time, and to resist Satan from stealing your seed.

Hebrews 6:11-12 says,

> *11 "And we desire that each one of you show the same diligence to the full assurance of hope until the end,*
>
> *12 that you do not become sluggish, but imitate those who through faith and patience inherit the promises."*

There is good news!

You may have been struggling with purpose for your life. Now God is saying to you that He not only has that purpose, hope or vision for you, but that His power is there to bring it to pass. Now that is good news!

Psalm 37 shows how hope, and desires come, and promises the power to bring them to pass.

First, He gives you the desires.

Psalm 37:4 says,

> *4 "Delight yourself also in the LORD, and He shall*

give you the desires of your heart."

I submit that the word *delight* here infers having an intimate relationship with the Lord. When you do that, the promise is that He will insert in you the desires He wants you to desire. I do not think it means that He will give you whatever you desire apart from what He puts in your heart, but rather, He will insert in you the power to desire what He wants for you. His desires will become your desires.

Then, He supplies the power.

Psalm 37:5 says,

5 "Commit your way to the LORD, Trust also in Him, and He shall bring it to pass."

Commit your way infers to live a life of loving obedience to the Lord. Then when you trust in that relationship and in His character, He will supply the power to bring your desires to pass. You do not have to have the power to live out your vision, your desire, and your dream! That is good news to those of us who know that we cannot make life work without Him. It gives real hope to the hopeless!

How did this work for Jacob's life?

Jacob had sown a lot of bad seeds in his life. He and his mom had deceived his father Isaac to receive the blessing of the first born from his brother Esau. Jacob had been a deceiver, and even though God's plan was for him to receive the blessing of the first-born, he had used ungodly principles to acquire it.

By time we catch up with him in Genesis chapters 30-31 he was reaping a lot of bad fruit. He had hooked up with his uncle Laban, who turned out to be more of a manipulator than Jacob had been. He fell in love with Rachel and made a deal with her father Laban to work for him for seven years in exchange for her hand in marriage. Laban tricked Jacob and substituted his more homely daughter Leah. Jacob made another deal to work an additional seven years for Rachel.

At the end of fourteen years God's plans for Jacob had come into their fullness of time, and He moved with His sovereignty to put them into place. This took place in spite of the bad seed he had sown and in spite of Satan's plans to steal the birthright from Jacob.

God gave Jacob a dream to get him to his purpose and destiny.

One of the ways the Holy Spirit creates pictures in our hearts is through dreams. Back in Jacob's time there was no written Word of God, and the Holy Spirit did not yet inhabit humans as a general rule. However God can still dispense dreams even today. He also gives us vision and hope through illuminating His written Word, visions by the Holy Spirit, and other means, in order to write upon the "tablets of our hearts," Proverbs 3:3 and 7:3.

Then this heart picture becomes our "hope" and the "desires of our hearts." We find ourselves wanting what God wants for our lives. It is safer to not always try to understand what God has for our future, because we can be self-deceived, interpreting God's hope for an ungodly carnal desire. It is safer to know that God has planted hope in our hearts, and then trust Him to bring it to pass with His power, leaving "our power" out of the picture. We don't need to "help" Him like Abraham did when Ishmael was conceived.

Many years ago I was having a conversation with the Lord while going for a long walk. I said, "Lord, please draw on the Tablet of my heart the vision you have for my life." He answered, "Larry, I don't need to draw My vision for you, It existed there before the foundation of the world." Then he quoted **Hebrews 4:3:**

> *"3 For we who have believed do enter that rest, as He has said: "So I swore in My wrath, 'They shall not enter My rest,'" although the works were finished from the foundation of the world."*

He said, " All we have to do is to scrape off the counterfeit vision that you, the World and Satan has drawn there." Many years ago before I even knew the Lord I met an artist in Washington D.C. who would go to museums and steal paintings, not for the painting but for the canvas. He would then paint his own work and cover up the original. God used this to give me understanding on this issue.

Years later as I was re-writing this chapter, The Lord asked me, "What was it that removed Jacob's counterfeit drawing on his Tablet?" I thought and answered, "His suffering?" "Right." He said.

The following is Jacob's dream. The merciful God intervened in Jacob's life.

Genesis 31:11-13 says,

> *11 "Then the Angel of God spoke to me in a dream, saying, 'Jacob.' And I said, 'Here I am.'*
>
> *12 And He said, 'Lift your eyes now and see, all the rams which leap on the flocks are streaked, speckled, and gray-spotted; for I have seen all that Laban is doing to you.*
>
> *13 I am the God of Bethel, where you anointed the pillar and where you made a vow to Me. Now arise, get out of this land, and return to the land of your family.'"*

Jacob made a deal with Laban as told in Genesis 30:25-43. He offered to work for Laban without specific wages, but that his compensation would only be the offspring of the cattle that had stripes and spots. To make it more interesting, Jacob agreed to move all the existing striped and spotted cattle three days journey from his ranch, and that he would only keep the solid color cattle. Laban could not understand how Jacob could breed cattle with stripes and spots if he only started with solid colors, so he quickly accepted the deal. It sounded impossible to Laban.

Jacob then proceeded to take poplar rods and carve spots and stripes on them. He put these rods in and around the watering troughs where only the strong cattle would water and feed. He did not put these rods where the weaker cattle would feed. Every time the cattle would drink and eat, they would also get the vision from the rods.

Genesis 31:4-10 says,

4 "So Jacob sent and called Rachel and Leah to the field, to his flock,

5 and said to them, 'I see your father's countenance, that it is not favorable toward me as before; but the God of my father has been with me.

6 And you know that with all my might I have served your father.

7 Yet your father has deceived me and changed my wages ten times, but God did not allow him to hurt me.

8 If he said thus: 'The speckled shall be your wages,' then all the flocks bore speckled. And if he said thus: 'The streaked shall be your wages,' then all the flocks bore streaked.

9 So God has taken away the livestock of your father and given them to me.

10 And it happened, at the time when the flocks conceived, that I lifted my eyes and saw in a dream, and behold, the rams which leaped upon the flocks were streaked, speckled, and gray-spotted.'"

Jacob became wealthy. His cattle began bringing forth offspring with stripes and spots in such great number that the Scripture says, "Thus the man became exceedingly prosperous, and had large flocks, female and male servants, and camels and donkeys" (Genesis 30:43). This could have only happened by a God miracle! This allowed Jacob to take his wives and leave Laban to return to his own land, to his destiny. I suggest that you read this entire story in Genesis chapters 30-31.

After this, Jacob proceeded to his encounter with his estranged brother Esau, and his wrestling encounter with God, where his name was changed to Israel.

It is comforting to know that if we stay in constant and intimate relationship with the Lord, keep our hearts right and allow

Him to plant His plans on our hearts, that He will rescue us from our detours in life and take us into our God-ordained purpose!

God wants us to be co-creators with Him.
He wanted the first Adam to be a co-creator, however Adam would not continue in the Word of God, but rather decided to produce his own hope and vision through his powerful mind.

The Power to Create.

Ephesians 5:1 (Amplified Bible) says,

"Therefore be imitators of God [copy Him and follow His example] as well-beloved children [imitate their father]."

Creating new things, changing old things. Because you and I are made in the image of God that's something we're always trying to do. But if we're to be successful at it, we need to learn a lesson about it from the Creator Himself, our very own heavenly Father.

In the original creation, God saw that what He originally created had become corrupt, and when He saw it He spoke out what His plan was. He did not speak what He saw; He spoke what He wanted it to be.

Genesis 1:1-3 says,

1 "In the beginning God created the heavens and the earth.

2 The earth was without form, and void; and darkness was on the face of the deep. And the Spirit of God was hovering over the face of the waters.

3 Then God said, 'Let there be light'; and there was light."

You know, He didn't just come upon creation by accident and say, "Well, what do you know! There's light!" No, before He began to recreate His universe, He first had a desired result (an inner idea, or image, of what He wanted to create) and then said, "Light be!" and light was.

His method of operation is stated in Romans 4:17, which says, "(as it is written, "I have made you a father of many nations") in the presence of Him whom he believed – God, who gives life to the dead and calls those things which do not exist as though they did."

As you continue in your authentic relationship with Jesus, you will discover a leading by Him, a guiding hand taking you into your purpose. You will discover desires and visions in your heart that were God given. You may not interpret them properly at first. However, God will smooth out the rough places and transform your mistakes and failures into your ordained path. This path will take you into your purpose. Be diligent and trust Him.

Understand however, that Satan will attempt to discourage you. He has some power to perpetuate the curse, to cause the bad seed of sin in your past and in the past of your ancestors, to manifest itself. While this is still being manifested in your life, you need to know what is going on. You need to know that God is turning your life around like He did Jacob's. You need to hang on to the promise, to the hope, so that in the end it will be real in your life's experience. Jesus became a curse for you so that you would inherit the blessings.

All of this is only possible because Jesus bore your curse on the Cross. Without that blood covenant exchange, you would be trapped in your own power to only bring your own man made plans to pass.

Your job during this period of hanging onto hope includes, your continually confessing the Word, the promise that God gave to you. It also includes speaking out in faith those Scriptures that apply generically.

Jacob believed the dream that God gave to him.

He believed it so much, that he cut spots and stripes into poplar rods and put them before the cattle so that they would prosper in their breeding.

In 1982 when I still had my grocery story and Jewish deli, and business was looking very bleak, I painted spots and stripes on some posts in the parking lot. I looked at them every day as I drove up to the store. Eventually God took me out of that business and put me in the business of His choice. Then, after many trials perpetrated by Satan and his associates, the new business prospered and still is to this date.

Hebrews 6:11-19 says,

11 "And we desire that each one of you show the same diligence to the full assurance of hope until the end,

12 that you do not become sluggish, but imitate those who through faith and patience inherit the promises.

13 For when God made a promise to Abraham, because He could swear by no one greater, He swore by Himself,

14 saying, 'Surely blessing I will bless you, and multiplying I will multiply you.'

15 And so, after he had patiently endured, he obtained the promise.

16 For men indeed swear by the greater, and an oath for confirmation is for them an end of all dispute.

17 Thus God, determining to show more abundantly to the heirs of promise the immutability of His counsel, confirmed it by an oath,

18 that by two immutable things, in which it is impossible for God to lie, we might have strong consolation, who have fled for refuge to lay hold of the hope set before us.

19 This hope we have as an anchor of the soul, both sure and steadfast, and which enters the Presence behind the veil."

You do that same, and you will inherit the promise.

End notes

[i]So why did Jesus make wine?

Here is my own personal opinion. I learned most of it from Dr. Carl Baugh, a Spirit filled scientist.

He said that before the flood in Noah's time, there was a firmament over the earth, which was an invisible globe made up of some sort of matter that kept the harmful rays of the sun from destroying things. It also had a metallic and crystal content that reflected the songs that the angels sang to the people on earth. It was like God's boom box! It had several other jobs. But at the flood this broke.

One of the things that the firmament prevented was the fermentation or death process of fruit. This fermentation is what creates alcohol. The alcohol does have some benefits like killing of germs, and in Bible days they would mix a little wine with some water for purification. But the priests who would minister in the presence of God were not allowed to drink any wine.

Notice, after the flood, Noah got drunk. I do not believe he did this on purpose; I feel like he was not aware of what happened.

I feel in the New Earth, that Jesus will give us the New Wine again, or the kind that does not have alcohol. This is different than grape juice, but it is something that we cannot imagine because we are living in a different earth now. I also believe that this original wine, and the New Wine is very tasty and healthy, but it does not have alcohol. Alcohol is made from a death process called fermentation and death is not from God.

In my opinion, the wine Jesus made that day was the wine of the new Kingdom of God, which is similar to the wine in the days before the flood. Before the flood the wine had no alcohol content (in my opinion) because fermentation, which was required, was not in existence as yet. Look at John 2:4 which demonstrates that this wine was indeed different.

John 2:4 (Amplified Bible) says,

10And said to him, Everyone else serves his best wine first, and when people have drunk freely, then he serves that which is not so good; but you have kept back the good wine until now!

Winkey Pratney on Alcohol. Taken from his article The Daniel Files

DRINKING

Minimize drug use of *any* kind. Find alternatives to what you have. Needless to say, you certainly cut out all illegal and legal *addictives*. Especially is this true with **alcohol** and **tobacco** of any kind.

More kids die by accident than any other cause of death among teenagers. Over *half* of those deaths are by drunk driving. More boys are murdered than kill themselves; drinking and drugs dominate in the cause of these deaths too. One single drink of alcohol *permanently kills off* an irreplaceable piece of brain.

All alcohols kill. Methyl blinds you as you die. Even a little propyl alcohol lets monsters loose in your body. But ethyl is the only one that kills you slow so you don't notice how you die.

Don't drink *don't drink at all.* Alcohol (the decayed end-product of rot) not only stuns your ability to think clearly, quickly and remember. Even small amounts knock out your ability to resist disease.

No wonder the Bible says, *"Wine is mocker, strong drink is raging and whoever is deceived by it is not wise."* (Prov. 20:1; Isa. 5:11,22; Isa. 28:7) No King's child is to touch alcohol. (Prov. 31:4) Wine is for no one in ministry (Lev. 10:9); you are to get your bravery, happiness, and loudness from the Holy Spirit! (Eph. 5:18; Acts 2:13)

The only legitimate use of strong drink in the Bible is *to dull the pain of someone who is dying*. (Prov. 31:6) Many kids use it just this same way today. On the cross, Jesus was offered a drug/alcohol mixture; He refused it.

www.ingramcontent.com/pod-product-compliance
Lightning Source LLC
LaVergne TN
LVHW020628100826
845148LV00012B/2098

* 9 7 8 0 9 6 7 6 7 3 1 8 9 *